WHAT IS THE BOOK OF PROVERBS?

Kids' Guides to God's Word Series

What Is the Book of Genesis?
What Is the Book of Exodus?
What Is the Book of Leviticus?
What Is the Book of Numbers?
What Is the Book of Deuteronomy?
What Is the Book of Joshua?
What Is the Book of Judges?
What Is the Book of Ruth?
What Is the Book of 1 Samuel?
What Is the Book of 2 Samuel?
What Is the Book of 1 Kings?
What Is the Book of 2 Kings?
What Are the Books of 1–2 Chronicles?
What Are the Books of Ezra & Nehemiah?
What Is the Book of Esther?
What Is the Book of Job?
What Is the Book of Psalms?
What Is the Book of Proverbs?
What Is the Book of Ecclesiastes?
What Are the Books of Song of Songs & Lamentations?
What Is the Book of Isaiah?
What Is the Book of Jeremiah?
What Is the Book of Ezekiel?
What Is the Book of Daniel?
What Are the Books of Hosea–Micah?
What Are the Books of Nahum–Malachi?

What Is the Gospel of Matthew?
What Is the Gospel of Mark?
What Is the Gospel of Luke?
What Is the Gospel of John?
What Is the Book of Acts?
What Is the Book of Romans?
What Is the Book of 1 Corinthians?
What Is the Book of 2 Corinthians?
What Is the Book of Galatians?
What Is the Book of Ephesians?
What Is the Book of Philippians?
What Are the Books of Colossians & Philemon?
What Are the Books of 1–2 Thessalonians?
What Are the Books of 1–2 Timothy & Titus?
What Is the Book of Hebrews?
What Is the Book of James?
What Are the Books of 1–2 Peter & Jude?
What Are the Books of 1-3 John?
What Is the Book of Revelation?

What Is the Book of
PROVERBS?

Michael Whitworth

ISBN 978-1-944704-83-4

Published by Start2Finish
Bend, Oregon 97702
start2finish.org

Printed in the United States of America
30 29 28 27 26   1 2 3 4 5

CONTENTS

INTRODUCTION

Every book in the Bible you've read so far has been a story. Genesis told the story of creation, the fall, and the family of Abraham. Exodus told the story of slavery and rescue. Joshua told the story of conquest. Judges told the story of failure. Ruth told a quiet love story. First Samuel told the story of kings. Even the laws in Leviticus were wrapped inside the story of Israel learning to live with a holy God.

Proverbs is different. There's no plot. No hero on a journey. No villain to defeat. No beginning, middle, and end. If the rest of the Bible is a movie, Proverbs is more like a coach pulling you aside before the game and saying, "Here's what you need to know to survive out there."

And honestly? That might make it the most useful book in the Bible for your life right now.

Because Proverbs is about the stuff you deal with every single day. What to do when your friend says something behind your back. How to handle money. Whether to speak up or stay quiet. How to tell the difference between someone who's good for you and someone who will drag you down. What to do with your anger. How to respond when you're wrong. Why laziness will cost you more than you think. What kind of person you're becoming based on the choices you make when nobody's watching.

The Bible's other books tell you what God has done. Proverbs tells you how to live in light of it.

THE WISEST MAN WHO EVER LIVED

To understand where Proverbs comes from, you need to know about Solomon. He was the son of King David and became king of Israel around 970 BC. When he took the throne, God appeared to him and offered him anything he wanted. Solomon didn't ask for wealth or power or a long life. He asked for wisdom. God was so pleased with the request that he gave Solomon wisdom beyond anything the world had ever seen, and then threw in the wealth and honor as a bonus.

First Kings says Solomon spoke three thousand proverbs. He studied plants and animals. Kings and queens traveled from distant nations just to hear him talk. He built the temple in Jerusalem. For a brief, shining moment, Israel was everything God had promised it could be.

But Solomon's story doesn't end well. The wisest man in the world married seven hundred wives, many of them from nations that worshiped other gods. Those marriages pulled his heart away from the Lord. By the end of his life, Solomon was building altars to foreign gods. The kingdom split apart after his death.

That's important to know because it tells you something about the book he left behind. Proverbs isn't the advice of a man who had it all figured out. It's the collected wisdom of someone who knew the truth but didn't always live it. The proverbs themselves are trustworthy. But the man who wrote most of them serves as a warning: knowing what's right and doing what's right are not the same thing.

HOW TO READ THIS BOOK

Here's the most important thing to understand before you start: proverbs are not promises.

When Proverbs says, "Train up a child in the way he should go, and when he is old he will not depart from it" (22:6), it's not guaranteeing that every well-raised kid turns out perfectly. When it says, "The Lord does not let the righteous go hungry" (10:3), it's not saying that no faithful person will ever miss a meal. Job and Ecclesiastes, two other wisdom books in the Bible, exist partly to push back against that kind of rigid reading.

Proverbs are principles. They describe how life generally works when all other things are equal. Hard work usually leads to prosperity. Laziness usually leads to poverty. Honesty usually builds trust. Lying usually destroys it. These are patterns built into the fabric of the world by the God who made it. They're reliable. But they're not formulas you can punch into a calculator and get a guaranteed result.

Read them as wisdom for navigating a complicated world, not as vending machine promises where you insert the right behavior and get the right outcome every time.

One more thing: the book has two very different halves. Chapters 1–9 contain long speeches from a father to his son, along with the dramatic appearances of a figure called Woman Wisdom, who calls out in the streets and invites people to choose life. These chapters read like a sermon. They build arguments. They develop ideas over multiple paragraphs.

Starting in chapter 10, everything changes. The long speeches disappear, replaced by hundreds of short, sharp, two-line sayings that cover every topic imaginable. These proverbs aren't arranged in any obvious order. Reading them is less like reading a book and more like opening a box of individually wrapped truths and examining them one at a time.

Both halves matter. The first half gives you the framework: fear God, pursue wisdom, avoid folly. The second half gives you the tools: specific observations about words, work, money, friendship, character, and justice that help you apply the framework to real life.

WHAT YOU'RE ABOUT TO READ

This book walks through Proverbs in eight chapters, following the shape of the biblical text:

The first two chapters cover Proverbs 1–9, the father's speeches and Wisdom's dramatic appeals. You'll learn why the fear of the Lord is the starting line, why the father warns about peer pressure before anything else, and why the book builds to a climactic scene where two women call out from the highest point of the city, each offering a meal and a future, and only one of them telling the truth.

The next five chapters are thematic, drawing from the hundreds of individual proverbs scattered across chapters 10–29. Each chapter gathers what Proverbs says about a single topic:

your words, your friends, your work and money, your character, and your commitment to justice and integrity.

The final chapter covers Proverbs 30–31, where two surprising voices close the book: a man named Agur, who begins by confessing how little he knows, and a poem about a woman whose life is the living portrait of everything Proverbs has been teaching.

WHY THIS MATTERS

You might be young. You might be reading this because someone handed it to you, or because it's part of a class, or because the cover looked interesting. Whatever brought you here, this book has something for you. Not because ancient proverbs are magically relevant, but because the things that trip people up haven't changed in three thousand years. We still struggle with pride. We still gossip. We still chase shortcuts. We still choose the wrong friends. We still say things we regret. We still want more than we need.

Proverbs meets you in all of those places. And it does something the rest of the Bible doesn't do in quite the same way: it sits down next to you in the ordinary moments of your Tuesday afternoon and says, "Here. This will help."

One more thing. The New Testament says that Jesus is "the wisdom of God" (1 Corinthians 1:24, 30). That means the wisdom you'll encounter in this book isn't just good advice from a clever king. It's a reflection of the character of God himself, and it finds its fullest expression in the person of Jesus. When Proverbs talks about wisdom being present at creation, laughing and delighting in the world God made, the early Christians read that and thought of Christ. When Proverbs says that finding wisdom means finding life, they heard an echo of Jesus saying, "I am the way, the truth, and the life."

Proverbs isn't just pointing you toward smarter decisions. It's pointing you toward a person.

But we're getting ahead of ourselves. First, we need to start where the book starts: with a father, a son, and the most important sentence in the entire book.

Turn the page.

1

THE STARTING LINE

Have you ever gotten advice you didn't want to hear? Maybe it was your mom telling you to stay away from a certain group of kids at school. Maybe it was your dad saying, "Think before you speak," right after you said something you couldn't take back. Maybe it was a coach pulling you aside and telling you that you weren't working hard enough, even though you thought you were doing fine.

In the moment, that kind of advice can feel annoying. Unnecessary. Like they don't understand your life. You hear the words, but something inside you resists them. You think, *I already know this.* Or, *That doesn't apply to me.* Or maybe just, *Leave me alone.*

But then a week later, or a month later, or sometimes years later, you realize they were right. The group of kids your mom warned you about got you into trouble. The words you didn't think about before speaking cost you a friendship. The coach was trying to help you get better, and you almost missed it because you didn't want to listen.

Here's what's interesting: the book of Proverbs opens with almost exactly that situation. A father is talking to his son. The son is young, probably a teenager, standing at the beginning of his adult life. And the father knows something the son doesn't: the choices he makes in the next few years will shape everything that follows. So the father speaks with an urgency that practically leaps off the page. He's not giving casual suggestions. He's pleading. He's warning. He's doing everything he can to get his son to pay attention before the stakes get real.

And then, right in the middle of the father's speech, another voice breaks in. A woman starts shouting in the streets. She's not whispering in a classroom or speaking softly in a living room. She's standing at the busiest intersection in the city, yelling over the noise of the crowd, calling out to anyone who will listen.

That woman is Wisdom. And she has something to say.

THE MOST IMPORTANT SENTENCE IN THE BOOK

Before the father gives a single piece of advice, before Wisdom makes her first speech, the book of Proverbs opens with a statement so important that everything else in the book depends on it.

"The fear of the Lord is the beginning of knowledge, but fools despise wisdom and discipline" (Proverbs 1:7).

That one sentence is the foundation of the entire book. It's like the first note in a piece of music that sets the key for everything that follows. If you miss this, you'll misread everything else.

But what does "the fear of the Lord" actually mean? It doesn't mean being terrified of God, like you'd be terrified of a bear charging at you. It means something closer to *taking God seriously.* It means recognizing that he is real, that he made the world, that he knows how life works, and that his opinion matters more than yours. It's the kind of respect that changes how you live, not because you're scared of getting punished, but because you understand that the God who created everything deserves to be listened to.

Think about it this way. If you knew absolutely nothing about the ocean and someone who had spent their whole life studying it offered to teach you how to navigate through it safely, you would be foolish to ignore them. Not because they're threatening you, but because they know things you don't, and your life might depend on what they have to say.

That's what the fear of the Lord is. It's the humility to say, "God knows more than I do, and I'm going to build my life on what he says." Without that starting point, Proverbs says, you can't even begin to become wise. You might become smart. You might become clever. But you won't become wise, because wisdom starts with knowing your place in the universe, and your place is not at the center of it. God is.

The opposite of this is what the book calls a "fool." In Proverbs, a fool isn't someone who can't learn. A fool is someone who *won't* learn. Someone who hears good advice and throws it away. Someone who thinks they already know everything they need to know. The fool's problem isn't a lack of intelligence. It's a refusal to listen.

That's the choice Proverbs puts in front of you before anything else. Will you be someone who listens? Or someone who doesn't?

THE FATHER'S WARNING

With that foundation laid, the father's teaching begins. And his first lesson might surprise you. He doesn't start with table manners or study habits. He starts with a warning about peer pressure.

"My son, if sinners entice you, do not give in to them" (1:10).

The picture he paints is vivid. He describes a group of people who invite the son to join them in violence and theft. "Come with us," they say. "We'll ambush someone. We'll fill our houses with stolen goods. Throw in your lot with us, and we'll share everything."

You might think, *I'm never going to join a gang of robbers.* And maybe not. But the father isn't just talking about literal crime. He's describing a pattern that shows up everywhere: the pull of a group that promises quick rewards if you'll just go along with what they're doing. Maybe it's a group at school that makes fun of other kids and wants you to join in. Maybe it's friends who pressure you into doing something you know is wrong because "everyone's doing it." Maybe it's a voice online that says you'll be accepted if you just follow the crowd, no matter where the crowd is going.

The promise is always the same: belong with us, and you'll get what you want.

But the father knows where this road leads. He uses a brilliant image: "How useless to spread a net in full view of all the birds!" (1:17). Even a bird has enough sense to avoid a trap it can see. But these people, blinded by greed, are walk-ing straight into a trap they've set for themselves. They think they're ambushing someone else, but they're destroying their own lives. "Such are the paths of everyone who is greedy for unjust gain," the father says. "It takes away the life of those who get it" (1:19).

The lesson is sharp and clear. The people who try hardest to take from others end up losing the most. Quick rewards that come at someone else's expense always cost you more than they give you.

THE WOMAN SHOUTING IN THE STREETS

Then something unexpected happens. The scene shifts from the quiet urgency of a father's voice to a woman shouting in the middle of the city.

"Wisdom calls aloud in the street; she raises her voice in the public squares. At the head of the noisy streets she cries out; in the gateways of the city she makes her speech" (1:20–21).

This is one of the most striking images in the Old Testament. Wisdom is described as a woman standing at the busiest, loudest, most crowded places in town, calling out to everyone who passes by. She's not hiding in a library. She's not waiting for people to come find her. She goes to where the people are, and she shouts to get their attention.

And her message isn't gentle. "How long will you who are simple love your simple ways? How long will mockers delight in mockery and fools hate knowledge?" (1:22).

There's frustration in her voice. She has been calling for a long time, and people have been ignoring her. She's been offering everything they need, and they've been walking right past her.

Then comes the warning. Wisdom says that the day is coming when the people who ignored her will face disaster. And when that day comes, they'll suddenly want her help. They'll cry out for wisdom. They'll look for answers. But it will be too late. "Then they will call to me but I will not answer; they will look for me but will not find me" (1:28).

That sounds harsh. But it's not cruelty. It's honesty. Wisdom is telling the truth about how life works: there are consequences to ignoring what is right, and those consequences don't wait forever. If you spend years refusing to listen, eventually you run out of time to learn.

But the speech doesn't end with judgment. It ends with a promise. "Whoever listens to me will live in safety and be at ease, without fear of harm" (1:33). The person who chooses to listen to Wisdom, the person who takes God seriously and builds their life on what is true, will have something the fool never has: peace.

SEEK IT LIKE BURIED TREASURE

Chapters 2–4 are the father's response to Wisdom's speech. It's as if he heard her shouting in the streets and turned to his son and said, "Did you hear that? *That* is what you need to go after."

What follows is one of the most passionate appeals in the entire Bible. The father tells his son to pursue wisdom the way you'd pursue the most valuable thing on earth. "If you look for it as for silver and search for it as for hidden treasure, then you will understand the fear of the Lord and find the knowledge of God. For the Lord gives wisdom; from his mouth come knowledge and understanding" (2:4-6).

Imagine someone told you there was a chest of gold buried somewhere in your backyard. Would you wander outside, glance around for a few seconds, and give up? Of course not. You'd dig up every inch of ground until you found it. That's the kind of energy the father says wisdom deserves. It's not something you stumble across while you're busy doing other things. It's something you go after with everything you have.

But here's what makes this different from a treasure hunt: the treasure is actually looking for *you* too. Wisdom is shouting in the streets. God gives wisdom to those who ask. The search isn't a shot in the dark. It's a response to someone who has already reached out.

And the rewards are staggering. The father says that wisdom will protect you. It will guard you from people who want to lead you astray (2:12). It will keep you on the right path when the wrong path looks easier (2:13–15). It will save you from decisions that seem exciting in the moment but lead to ruin (2:16–19).

In chapter 3, the father raises the stakes even higher. "Trust in the Lord with all your heart and lean not on your own understanding; in all your ways submit to him, and he will make your paths straight" (3:5–6). That might be the most famous passage in the entire book, and it says something that everyone needs to hear: you don't have to figure everything out on your own. In fact, you *can't* figure everything out on your own. But if you trust God instead of insisting on your own way, he will guide you.

Then comes a description of wisdom that sounds almost like a fairy tale. Wisdom holds long life in one hand and riches and honor in the other (3:16). She offers pleasant paths and peace (3:17). She is called "a tree of life to those who take hold of her" (3:18), an image that reaches all the way back to the Garden of Eden, where Adam and Eve once had access to the tree of life before sin separated them from God.

The point is clear. Wisdom isn't just useful. Wisdom is life itself. And the way you get it hasn't changed: you fear the Lord, you listen to instruction, and you pursue wisdom like it's the most valuable thing in the world. Because it is.

GUARD YOUR HEART

Chapter 4 closes this opening section with one of the most personal moments in the book. The father tells his son that he himself was once a young man, sitting at his own father's feet, hearing these same words. "When I was a boy in my father's house, still tender, and an only child of my mother, he taught me and said, 'Take hold of my words with all your heart; keep my commands and you will live'" (4:3–4).

This is a chain that goes back through generations. A grandfather teaching a father. A father teaching a son. The same truth, passed down through a family like an inheritance more valuable than land or money.

And then the father gives his son a command that Jesus himself would echo centuries later: "Above all else, guard your heart, for everything you do flows from it" (4:23).

Your heart, in the Bible, doesn't mean your emotions. It means the core of who you are, the place where your thoughts, desires, and decisions come from. Everything you say, every-thing you do, every choice you make flows from that center. If your heart is filled with wisdom and the fear of the Lord, your life will reflect it. If your heart is filled with foolishness and selfishness, your life will reflect that instead.

Guard it. Protect it. Be careful what you let in. Because what gets into your heart eventually comes out in your life.

WHAT THIS MEANS FOR US

First, wisdom starts with humility, not intelligence. You don't need to be the smartest person in the room to be wise. You need to be someone who listens. The fear of the Lord is the starting line, and anyone can stand there. All it takes is the willingness to admit that God knows more than you do.

Second, the people you listen to will shape who you become. The father's very first warning is about the voices his son will hear once he leaves home. Some voices will promise quick rewards. Others will offer something slower but lasting. Wisdom says: pay attention to who is talking, and ask yourself where their advice will actually lead you.

Third, wisdom doesn't hide from you, but it does require effort. Wisdom is shouting in the streets. God gives wisdom to those who ask. But you still have to pursue it like hidden treasure. You have to read, listen, think, and choose. Wisdom won't force itself on you. It invites, and you decide whether to accept.

Fourth, guard your heart. What you let into the center of who you are will determine the direction of your whole life. That means being intentional about what you watch, what you listen to, who you spend time with, and what you allow to shape your thinking. Not because those things are always dangerous, but because your heart is always absorbing something. Make sure it's absorbing the right things.

TALKING POINTS

1. **Proverbs says "the fear of the Lord is the beginning of knowledge."** What do you think it looks like to "fear God" in everyday life? How is that different from just being scared of God?

2. **The father warns his son about people who promise quick rewards in exchange for doing wrong.** Where do you see this kind of pressure in your own life? What makes it hard to say no when a group is pressuring you to go along?

3. **Wisdom is described as a woman shouting in the streets, trying to get people's attention.** Why do you think people ignore wisdom even when it's right in front of them? When have you ignored good advice and later wished you hadn't?

4. **Proverbs 2:4 says to search for wisdom "as for hidden treasure."** What does that kind of effort look like in real life? What's one thing you could do this week to actively pursue wisdom instead of just hoping it shows up?

5. **"Above all else, guard your heart, for everything you do flows from it" (4:23).** What are some things that influence your heart every day, for better or worse? How can you be more intentional about protecting what gets in?

The father has laid the foundation. Wisdom has made her first speech. The starting line has been drawn, and you've been invited to step up to it. But Proverbs isn't done with you yet. In the next few chapters, the stakes get higher. Two voices will call to you, each one promising to give you what you need. One of them is telling the truth. The other one will destroy you. And you'll have to decide which one to follow.

Turn the page.

2

TWO VOICES CALLING

Robert Louis Stevenson wrote a story in 1886 called *The Strange Case of Dr. Jekyll and Mr. Hyde*. It's about a respected London doctor named Henry Jekyll who discovers a potion that splits him into two people. When he drinks it, he transforms into Edward Hyde, a cruel, violent man with no conscience and no restraint. At first, Jekyll thinks he can control it. He'll be the good doctor by day and let Hyde out only when he wants to. He tells himself it's harmless. He can stop whenever he chooses.

He can't.

Over time, Hyde grows stronger. The transformations start happening without the potion. Jekyll begins losing control of when Hyde appears and what Hyde does. The man who thought he could manage both lives discovers that the darker voice doesn't stay in its corner. It takes over. By the end of the story, Jekyll is gone. Hyde is all that's left.

Stevenson's story has haunted readers for over a century because it tells a truth everyone recognizes: there are two voices inside every person. One pulls you toward what is good, honest, and life-giving. The other pulls you toward what feels exciting but leads somewhere dark. And the voice you feed is the one that grows stronger.

That's exactly what Proverbs 5–9 is about. These chapters are the climax of the father's teaching, and they build to the most dramatic scene in the entire book. Two women stand on the highest point of the city. Both call out to the same young man. Both offer a meal. Both promise something good. One of them is telling the truth. The other will destroy him.

The question is whether he can tell the difference.

THE VOICE THAT LIES

Before the father introduces the two women directly, he spends three chapters warning his son about a specific danger: the voice that sounds sweet but leads to ruin.

In chapters 5–7, the father describes a woman who flatters, seduces, and ultimately destroys the men who follow her. She speaks with smooth words. She makes promises that sound wonderful. She presents herself as exciting, glamorous, and irresistible. Everything about her initial appearance says, "This is what you've been looking for."

But the father pulls back the curtain and shows his son what's actually happening.

"Her lips drip honey, and her speech is smoother than oil; but in the end she is bitter as gall, sharp as a double-edged sword. Her feet go down to death; her steps lead straight to the grave" (5:3–5).

The image is jarring on purpose. Honey and oil on the outside. Death on the inside. The father is telling his son that the most dangerous things in life don't announce themselves as dangerous. They come disguised as something desirable.

Chapter 7 is even more vivid. The father describes watching from his window as a young man walks past a certain woman's house at twilight. The young man isn't planning to do anything wrong. He's just wandering, killing time, not really thinking. But she's been waiting. She comes out dressed to attract attention, speaks flattering words, and invites him inside. "Come, let's drink deeply of love," she says (7:18). The young man follows her. And the father's commentary is devastating:

"All at once he followed her like an ox going to the slaughter, like a deer stepping into a noose, like a bird darting into a snare, little knowing it will cost him his life" (7:22–23).

He didn't see the trap because he wasn't looking for one.

Now, depending on how old you are, some of this might feel like it doesn't apply to you yet. That's okay. But here's what the father is really teaching, and it goes far beyond romance. He's teaching his son a principle that applies to every area of life: *some of the worst decisions you'll ever make will feel good at first.* The voice that leads you off course won't sound evil. It will sound fun, exciting, easy, or perfectly reasonable. It will tell you what you want to hear. And if you're not paying attention, if you're just wandering without thinking, you'll follow it before you realize where it's taking you.

The father is teaching his son to think about where a path leads, not just how it looks at the starting line.

T

HE BETTER PATH

But the father doesn't just warn. He also shows his son what the right path looks like, and he makes it sound beautiful.

In chapter 5, after warning about the danger of the wrong relationship, the father turns around and paints a vivid picture of what a faithful, committed marriage looks like. "Rejoice in the wife of your youth," he says (5:18). He describes marital love with warmth and tenderness, using images of flowing water and springs and satisfaction. The point is clear: God designed something good. The counterfeits are dangerous precisely because they imitate something that, in its proper place, is wonderful.

Chapter 6 adds a rapid-fire collection of practical warnings. The father addresses everything from foolish financial decisions (don't pledge money you can't afford to lose) to laziness (go watch the ants and learn something) to dishonesty (God hates a lying tongue). Right in the middle, he lists seven things the Lord detests: proud eyes, a lying tongue, hands that shed innocent blood, a heart that plots evil, feet that rush toward wrong, a false witness, and anyone who stirs up conflict among friends (6:16–19).

Read that list again. It's a portrait of the kind of person the father is begging his son not to become. Every item on the list is a character flaw, not a single event. Proud eyes. A plotting heart. Feet that rush toward wrong. The father is saying that foolishness isn't just about one bad decision. It's about the kind of person you're becoming, one choice at a time.

WISDOM TELLS HER STORY

Then chapter 8 changes everything. The scene shifts from the father's voice to Wisdom's voice, and this time she doesn't just call out a warning like she did in chapter 1. She tells her story. She reveals who she is. And what she says is breathtaking.

First, she establishes her character. "I speak the truth," she says. "My lips detest wickedness. All the words of my mouth are just; none of them is crooked or perverse" (8:7–8). She is associated with good judgment, knowledge, and discretion. Kings reign by her. Rulers make just laws because of her. She hates pride, arrogance, and evil behavior.

Then she makes a claim that elevates the entire book to a different level. "The Lord brought me forth as the first of his works, before his deeds of old; I was formed long ages ago, at the very beginning, when the world came to be" (8:22–23).

Wisdom was there before anything else existed. Before the oceans, before the mountains, before the sky was set in place, Wisdom was already present with God. And she wasn't just watching. She was active, participating in the creation of the world itself.

"I was there when he set the heavens in place, when he marked out the horizon on the face of the deep. … Then I was constantly at his side. I was filled with delight day after day, rejoicing always in his presence, rejoicing in his whole world and delighting in the human race" (8:27, 30–31).

Picture that scene. God is creating the universe, and Wisdom is right beside him, laughing, celebrating, delighting in every act of creation. There is joy here. There is play. The God who made the stars and the seas did it with wisdom, and that wisdom was filled with gladness.

This matters because it tells you something about the universe you live in. The world wasn't thrown together randomly. It was crafted with wisdom, and that wisdom still holds it together. When you live wisely, you're not following an arbitrary set of rules. You're living in harmony with the way the world was actually made. You're moving with the grain of the universe instead of against it.

And then Wisdom makes her appeal. "Now then, my children, listen to me; blessed are those who keep my ways. Listen to my instruction and be wise; do not disregard it. … For those who find me find life and receive favor from the Lord. But those who fail to find me harm themselves; all who hate me love death" (8:32–33, 35–36).

There it is. Find Wisdom, find life. Reject Wisdom, choose death. The stakes could not be higher.

TWO BANQUETS

Now comes the scene the entire first section of Proverbs has been building toward. Chapter 9 opens with Wisdom preparing a feast, and it closes with another woman doing the same thing. The contrast is deliberate, dramatic, and impossible to miss.

Wisdom has built a magnificent house with seven pillars. She has prepared a lavish banquet: meat, wine, a table set and ready. She sends out her servants to the highest point of the city and calls to everyone passing by: "Let all who are simple come to my house! Come, eat my food and drink the wine I have mixed. Leave your simple ways and you will live; walk in the way of insight" (9:4–6).

Everything about this invitation is generous, public, and honest. The house is grand. The food is prepared. The offer is free. And the promise is life.

Then, at the end of the chapter, another woman appears. Her name is Folly, and the description is deliberately written to mirror Wisdom's invitation, point by point.

"Folly is an unruly woman; she is simple and knows nothing. She sits at the door of her house, on a seat at the highest point of the city, calling out to those who pass by, who go straight on their way: 'Let all who are simple come to my house!' To those who have no sense she says, 'Stolen water is sweet; food eaten in secret is delicious!'" (9:13–17).

Did you catch it? Folly sits at the same location as Wisdom: the highest point of the city. In the ancient world, that was where the temple stood. Both women claim to speak with divine authority. Both call out to the same people. Both use almost identical words: "Let all who are simple come to my house."

But look at the differences.

Wisdom built her house. Folly just sits at the door of hers. Wisdom prepared a feast with care and effort. Folly offers stolen water and secret food. Wisdom's invitation is public and open. Folly's appeal is to secrecy and what's forbidden. Wisdom promises life. Folly doesn't mention what's waiting inside her house.

The narrator does, though. The chapter ends with one of the most chilling sentences in the Old Testament: "But little do they know that the dead are there, that her guests are in the depths of the grave" (9:18).

The men who accepted Folly's invitation are already dead. They just don't know it yet.

THE CHOICE

This is the scene the father has been preparing his son for all along. Two voices. Two invitations. Two tables. Two outcomes. And the young man walking down the street has to choose.

What makes the choice so difficult is that both voices sound appealing. Folly doesn't announce herself as death. She announces herself as pleasure, excitement, and freedom from rules. Her pitch is simple: what's forbidden tastes better. Stolen water is sweeter than the kind you're allowed to drink. Life is more fun when nobody's watching.

Wisdom's pitch is different. She offers something real, something lasting, something built on truth. But it requires humility. It requires discipline. It requires admitting that you don't already know everything and that your own instincts aren't always trustworthy. Wisdom's feast is better in every way, but you have to be willing to sit down at her table and learn.

The father has done everything he can. He has warned, pleaded, described, and illustrated. He has shown his son what's behind both doors. Now the son has to decide.

And so do you. Every day, in ways large and small, you hear both voices. One says, "Take the shortcut. Nobody will know. You deserve this. Rules are for other people." The other says, "Think about where this leads. Choose what's true even when it's harder. Build something that lasts."

The voice you listen to today shapes the person you become tomorrow.

WHAT THIS MEANS FOR US

First, the most dangerous lies sound like the truth. Folly doesn't wear a sign that says "I will ruin your life." She dresses up like something good. The father's whole strategy in these chapters is to teach his son to look past the surface. Don't just ask "Does this feel good right now?" Ask "Where does this lead?" That question will save you more times than you can count.

Second, secrecy is a warning sign. Folly's big selling point is that her food is eaten in secret. Whenever a voice tells you that something is fine as long as nobody finds out, pay attention. That's not freedom. That's a trap. Things that are genuinely good don't need to hide.

Third, Wisdom was there before anything else. She isn't a set of rules someone invented to keep you from having fun. She is woven into the fabric of the universe. When you live wisely, you're living the way the world was designed to work. When you reject wisdom, you're fighting against reality itself, and reality always wins.

Fourth, both voices call to the same people. You don't have to be especially foolish to fall for Folly's invitation. She targets everyone, including people who are already on the right path (9:15). The difference between the wise and the foolish isn't that the wise never hear the wrong voice. It's that they've trained themselves to recognize it and walk the other way.

TALKING POINTS

1. **The father describes the deceptive voice as sounding like honey and feeling like oil, but ending in bitterness and death.** Can you think of examples from real life where something seemed amazing at first but turned out to be harmful? What made it hard to see the truth at the beginning?

2. **In chapter 7, the young man who gets into trouble isn't planning to do anything wrong. He's just wandering without thinking.** Why is aimlessness dangerous? How does having a clear sense of direction protect you from bad decisions?

3. **Wisdom says she was present at creation, laughing and delighting in God's work.** What does this tell you about the nature of wisdom? How does it change the way you think about following God's guidance if wisdom isn't just a set of restrictions but something joyful?

4. **Wisdom and Folly both call from the highest point of the city and say almost the same words.** If they sound so similar, how can you learn to tell the difference between the two? What clues does the text give you?

5. **Folly's sales pitch is "Stolen water is sweet; food eaten in secret is delicious."** Why do you think forbidden things sometimes feel more exciting? What's the problem with making decisions based on that feeling?

The table is set. Two invitations have been given. The first nine chapters of Proverbs have laid the foundation: fear the Lord, pursue wisdom like treasure, guard your heart, and choose the right voice when both are calling your name. Now the book shifts. Starting in chapter 10, Proverbs moves from long speeches to short, sharp sayings that cover every corner of life. The father has given his son the framework. The proverbs that follow are the tools.

Turn the page.

3

WATCH YOUR MOUTH

Disney's *Bambi* has a scene that almost everyone remembers, even if they haven't seen the movie. Young Thumper the rabbit is chattering away, making fun of Bambi for being clumsy on the ice. His mother stops him and asks, "What did your father tell you this morning?" Thumper hangs his head, shuffles his feet, and mumbles, "If you can't say something nice, don't say nothing at all."

It's one of the most quoted lines in movie history. It gets printed on classroom posters and stitched into decorative pillows. And honestly? It's pretty good advice. But the book of Proverbs would say it doesn't go nearly far enough.

Proverbs doesn't just tell you to avoid saying mean things. It says your words have the power to give life or cause death. Not figuratively. Not as an exaggeration. As a statement about how reality works.

"The tongue has the power of life and death" (18:21).

That's not a suggestion. It's a warning. And if you're navigating group chats and hallway conversations, figuring out who to trust and what to say when you're angry or hurt or trying to fit in, this might be the most practical chapter in the entire book. Because Proverbs has more to say about your words than almost any other topic.

WORDS ARE NOT JUST WORDS

We live in a world that likes to say "they're just words." Someone insults you, and people say, "Don't let it bother you. It's just talk." Someone lies about you, and the advice is, "Ignore it. Words can't hurt you."

Proverbs disagrees. Completely. "Reckless words pierce like a sword, but the tongue of the wise brings healing" (12:18).

Notice the comparison. Reckless words don't just annoy. They don't just sting a little. They *pierce*. They cut into you the way a weapon does. And if you've ever had someone say something cruel about you, especially someone you trusted, you know this is true. You can still remember the words years later. They left a wound.

But the second half of the proverb is just as important: the tongue of the wise *brings healing*. Words don't just destroy. They also repair. They encourage. They comfort. They tell people the truth they need to hear at the moment they need to hear it. The same mouth that can wound can also heal. The question Proverbs keeps asking is: which one will yours do?

"The mouth of the righteous is a fountain of life" (10:11). A fountain doesn't just produce water once and stop. It keeps flowing. It refreshes everyone who comes near it. That's what the speech of a wise person does: it sustains and strengthens the people around them.

On the other hand: "The mouth of a fool invites ruin" (10:14). The fool's words don't just fail to help. They actively attract disaster, for the fool and for everyone nearby.

Your words, Proverbs is saying, are not neutral. They are always doing something. Building up or tearing down. Healing or wounding. Giving life or dealing death. There is no such thing as "just words."

THE POWER OF FEWER WORDS

One of the most consistent themes in Proverbs is this: wise people talk less than you'd expect. "When words are many, sin is not absent, but whoever holds their tongue is wise" (10:19).

Think about that for a moment. The more you talk, the more likely you are to say something you shouldn't. This isn't because speaking is bad. It's because most people don't think before they speak, and the more words that come out, the greater the chance that something careless, hurtful, or untrue slips through.

Proverbs takes this idea and sharpens it to a razor's edge: "Even fools are thought wise if they keep silent, and discerning if they hold their tongues" (17:28). That's almost funny. A fool who says nothing looks smarter than a fool who opens his mouth. Silence, in other words, is always an option, and it's almost always safer than speaking without thinking.

"Those who guard their lips preserve their lives, but those who speak rashly will come to ruin" (13:3). The contrast is blunt. Guard your lips, and you protect yourself. Speak without thinking, and you invite destruction. The ancient world understood something that the age of instant messaging makes easy to forget: once words leave your mouth, or once you hit send, you cannot take them back. Ever.

This doesn't mean you should never speak. Proverbs values good speech enormously. But it insists that the wise person thinks carefully about what to say, when to say it, and whether it needs to be said at all. In a world that rewards the loudest voice and the fastest reply, Proverbs quietly says: the wisest person in the room might be the one who hasn't spoken yet.

WHAT COMES OUT REVEALS WHAT'S INSIDE

Proverbs draws a direct line between your heart and your mouth. What you say reveals who you are.

"The tongue of the righteous is choice silver, but the heart of the wicked is of little value" (10:20). Notice how the proverb pairs tongue and heart. The righteous person's speech is valuable because it flows from a heart shaped by wisdom. The wicked person's heart is worthless, and their words prove it.

This works in both directions. Your words reveal what's already inside you, and the words you keep repeating gradually shape what's inside you even further. If you make a habit of complaining, your heart becomes a complaining heart. If you make a habit of lying, even about small things, you become a person for whom lies come naturally. If you train yourself to speak with encouragement and honesty, those qualities take root deeper in your character.

Jesus would later make this principle explicit: "Out of the overflow of the heart, the mouth speaks" (Matthew 12:34). But the idea comes straight from Proverbs. Your mouth is a window into your heart. If you want to know what kind of person you're becoming, listen to the words that come out of you when you're not thinking about it. That's the real you talking.

THE GENTLE ANSWER

One of the most famous proverbs in the entire book is also one of the hardest to practice. "A gentle answer turns away wrath, but a harsh word stirs up anger" (15:1).

Everyone knows this is true. When someone comes at you with anger and you respond calmly, the temperature drops. When someone comes at you and you fire back with something sharp, the whole situation explodes. You've seen it happen in arguments between friends, between siblings, in classrooms, and online.

But knowing it and doing it are two completely different things. When someone is rude to you, every instinct in your body tells you to be rude back. When someone raises their voice, you want to raise yours louder. Responding gently when someone is attacking you requires a kind of strength that most people underestimate. It's not weakness. It's self-control, and Proverbs treats self-control as one of the highest marks of wisdom.

"A person's wisdom yields patience, and it is to their glory to overlook an offense" (19:11). The wise person doesn't have to respond to every insult, answer every accusation, or win every argument. Sometimes the strongest thing you can do is let it go. That doesn't mean you become a doormat. Proverbs also says, "Better is open rebuke than hidden love" (27:5). There are times when the right thing to do is speak up directly, even when it's uncomfortable. But the wise person knows the difference between a fight worth having and one that will only make things worse.

THE GOSSIP PROBLEM

If Proverbs has a least favorite sin when it comes to speech, it might be gossip. "A gossip betrays a confidence, but a trustworthy person keeps a secret" (11:13). "The words of a gossip are like choice morsels; they go down to the inmost parts" (18:8).

That second proverb is disturbingly accurate. Gossip doesn't just float on the surface. It sinks in. When someone tells you something juicy about another person, you can feel how satisfying it is to hear it. It's like a delicious snack, and once it's inside you, it's hard to get rid of. You carry it around. You want to share it with someone else. Before long, a story that may not even be true has spread through an entire group and done real damage to a real person.

Proverbs 26:20 uses an image that's simple but devastating: "Without wood a fire goes out; without a gossip a quarrel dies down." Gossip is the fuel that keeps conflict burning. Remove the gossip, and the fire dies on its own. Every time you choose not to repeat something you've heard about someone else, you're starving a fire of its fuel. Every time you pass it along, you're throwing another log on.

This is especially relevant in a world of group chats and social media, where information travels faster than anyone can verify it and where screenshots can destroy a reputation in minutes. The technology is new. The temptation is ancient. And Proverbs' answer hasn't changed: a trustworthy person keeps a confidence. Full stop.

LIES AND THEIR COST

Proverbs doesn't treat lying as a minor offense. It treats it as something God personally hates.

In the list of seven things the Lord detests (6:16–19), two of the seven are directly about dishonest speech: "a lying tongue" and "a false witness who pours out lies." God takes lying seriously because lies destroy the trust that holds communities together. When people can't trust each other's words, everything falls apart: friendships, families, churches, and governments.

"Lying lips conceal hate, and those who spread slander are fools" (10:18). The liar's problem isn't just that they say untrue things. It's that lying is a form of violence against the people who trust you. When you lie to someone, you're treating their trust as something you're willing to sacrifice for your own benefit. And Proverbs says that makes you a fool, no matter how clever the lie.

"Truthful lips endure forever, but a lying tongue lasts only a moment" (12:19). Lies have a shelf life. They get discovered. They collapse under their own weight. But truth endures. The person who builds a reputation on honesty will have that reputation long after the clever liar's stories have fallen apart.

THE RIGHT WORD AT THE RIGHT TIME

Proverbs doesn't just warn about the dangers of speech. It also celebrates the beauty of words used well.

"A word aptly spoken is like apples of gold in settings of silver" (25:11). Imagine a piece of jewelry so perfectly crafted that it catches your eye and holds it. That's what the right word at the right time is like. It's not just helpful. It's beautiful. It's the kind of thing that makes you stop and say, "That was exactly what I needed to hear."

"Gracious words are a honeycomb, sweet to the soul and healing to the bones" (16:24). Good words don't just sound pleasant. They heal. They nourish. They strengthen people from the inside out.

And then there's this: "The lips of the righteous nourish many" (10:21). The wise person's words don't just benefit one person. They feed whole communities. Think of a teacher who knows exactly how to explain something so that it clicks. Think of a friend who says the one sentence that pulls you out of a bad place. Think of a parent who tells you the truth when you need to hear it, even though it's hard. Those words do something. They give life. And according to Proverbs, that's exactly what your words were designed to do.

WHAT THIS MEANS FOR US

First, your words are doing more than you think. Every conversation, every text, every comment is either building someone up or tearing someone down. There's no neutral gear. Proverbs asks you to take your speech as seriously as you'd take any other major decision in your life, because that's how seriously God takes it.

Second, learn the discipline of silence. You don't have to respond to everything. You don't have to have the last word. You don't have to fill every silence with noise. Sometimes the wisest thing you can do is close your mouth and wait. The fool speaks first and thinks later. The wise person reverses the order.

Third, refuse to be a gossip. It will cost you nothing to keep someone else's secret. It will cost you nothing to decide not to repeat a rumor. But it may cost someone everything if you don't. Be the kind of person who can be trusted with information. That reputation is worth more than the momentary thrill of having something interesting to share.

Fourth, tell the truth. Always. Even when it's uncomfortable, even when a lie would be easier, even when the truth makes you look bad. A reputation for honesty is one of the most valuable things you can build, and every lie, no matter how small, chips away at it.

Fifth, use your words to heal. You have the ability to encourage, comfort, and strengthen the people around you. Don't waste it. A single sentence spoken at the right moment can change someone's entire day, and sometimes their entire life. Proverbs says the mouth of the righteous is a fountain of life. Be a fountain.

TALKING POINTS

1. **Proverbs says "the tongue has the power of life and death."** Can you think of a time when someone's words gave you life, whether it was encouragement, comfort, or truth you needed to hear? What about a time when words caused real damage?

2. **"When words are many, sin is not absent."** Why do you think talking too much leads to problems? How can you get better at pausing and thinking before you speak, especially when you're emotional?

3. **Gossip is compared to "choice morsels" that go deep inside you.** Why do you think gossip feels so satisfying to hear,

even though we know it's wrong? What strategies can help you stop a gossip chain instead of continuing it?

4. **"A gentle answer turns away wrath, but a harsh word stirs up anger." Think of a recent conflict you witnessed or were involved in.** How might a gentle response have changed the outcome? What makes it so hard to respond gently when someone is being harsh?

5. **Proverbs celebrates the beauty of "a word aptly spoken" and "gracious words" that heal like a honeycomb.** Who is someone in your life whose words consistently build you up? What can you learn from the way they speak?

The proverbs about words could fill a book all by themselves. But the message comes down to something simple enough for anyone to understand and hard enough that even the wisest people work at it their whole lives. Your mouth is the most powerful tool you own. It can heal or destroy, build trust or shatter it, give life or deal death. Every day you get to choose which one it will be.

Turn the page.

4

CHOOSE YOUR FRIENDS

Think about the lunch table you sit at every day. That might sound like a strange place to start a chapter about ancient wisdom, but stay with me. The lunch table is one of the most important decisions you make, and you probably don't even think of it as a decision. You just sit down. But the people you sit with shape the conversation. The conversation shapes your thinking. Your thinking shapes your choices. And your choices shape your life.

Maybe you sit with people who make you laugh, challenge you to think, and have your back when things get hard. Or maybe you sit with people who spend the whole time tearing other people apart, pressuring you to go along with things you know are wrong, or making you feel like you have to be someone you're not just to belong.

Either way, those thirty minutes a day are doing something to you. Slowly, almost invisibly, the people you spend the most time with are turning you into someone. The question is: who?

The book of Proverbs would tell you that this is one of the most important questions you will ever answer. Not "What career should I choose?" Not "Where should I live?" But "Who am I walking with?" Because Proverbs is convinced that the people around you will determine the direction of your life more than almost any other single factor.

THE PROVERB THAT EXPLAINS EVERYTHING

If you had to pick one verse that captures what Proverbs teaches about friendship, it would be this: "Walk with the wise and become wise, for a companion of fools suffers harm" (13:20).

Read that again. It's not complicated. It doesn't need a college degree to understand. But it might be the most practical sentence in the entire Bible.

The people you walk with shape who you become. If you spend your time around wise people, people who fear God, tell the truth, work hard, and treat others well, those qualities will rub off on you. You'll start thinking the way they think, talking the way they talk, and making decisions the way they make decisions. Not because you're copying them, but because wisdom is contagious. It spreads from person to person like warmth from a fire.

But the reverse is also true. If you spend your time around fools, people who mock what is good, take shortcuts, lie when it's convenient, and live only for themselves, their foolishness will seep into you. You won't even notice it happening at first. You'll laugh at jokes you used to find mean. You'll start bending rules you used to respect. You'll slowly become the kind of person you never planned to be.

And notice the last word of the proverb: *harm*. The companion of fools doesn't just miss out on wisdom. They get hurt.

Foolish friends don't leave you where they found you. They drag you somewhere worse.

THE FRIENDS YOU NEED

Proverbs doesn't just warn you about bad friends. It paints a vivid picture of what good friendship looks like, and it's nothing like what most people think. "As iron sharpens iron, so one person sharpens another" (27:17).

This is one of the most quoted verses in the book, and for good reason. Picture a blacksmith running one piece of iron against another. It's not gentle. There's friction. There's heat. Sparks fly. But the result is a sharper edge, a better tool, something more useful and effective than it was before.

That's what real friendship does. A true friend doesn't just tell you what you want to hear. A true friend makes you better. They challenge your thinking. They call you out when you're wrong. They push you to grow in ways you wouldn't push yourself. It's not always comfortable, but it produces something valuable.

This is exactly why Proverbs says something that sounds harsh until you think about it: "Wounds from a friend can be trusted, but an enemy multiplies kisses" (27:6). A real friend will sometimes say things that sting. They'll tell you the truth about yourself when you'd rather not hear it. And those "wounds" are trustworthy because they come from someone who actually cares about your future, not just your feelings in the moment.

An enemy, on the other hand, will flatter you. They'll tell you everything is fine. They'll "kiss" you with approval and agreement because they don't care enough to risk the relationship by telling you the truth. Flattery feels better than honesty. But flattery leaves you exactly where you are, while honest correction moves you forward.

This is why Proverbs also says, "Better is open rebuke than hidden love" (27:5). Love that never speaks up isn't really doing its job. If someone sees you heading toward a cliff and says nothing because they don't want to upset you, that's not love. That's cowardice dressed up as kindness.

THE FRIENDS YOU NEED TO AVOID

Proverbs is equally direct about the kind of people you should stay away from. "Do not make friends with a hot-tempered person, do not associate with one easily angered, or you may learn their ways and get yourself ensnared" (22:24–25).

Notice the reasoning. The danger isn't just that an angry person might hurt you directly, though that's certainly possible. The deeper danger is that you'll *learn their ways*. You'll start reacting to frustration the way they do. You'll pick up their habits of blowing up, holding grudges, and treating anger as an acceptable way to handle every problem. Behavior is contagious. Proverbs knows this, and it warns you to be careful about what you're catching.

The same principle applies more broadly: "Stay away from a fool, for you will not find knowledge on their lips" (14:7). A fool, in Proverbs, isn't someone who is unintelligent. A fool is someone who refuses to learn, who mocks wisdom, who has no interest in doing what is right. Spending time with such a person is a waste at best and dangerous at worst, because they have nothing to give you except their foolishness.

"The violent entice their neighbors and make them walk on a path that is not good" (16:29). This echoes the very first lesson the father taught his son back in chapter 1, when he warned about the gang that says, "Come with us." Bad company doesn't just exist alongside you. It actively pulls you in a direction. It recruits. It makes the wrong path look appealing. And if you aren't grounded in wisdom before the invitation comes, you might not recognize what's happening until you're already in too deep.

WHAT FRIENDSHIP COSTS

One of the things Proverbs reveals about friendship is that real loyalty has a price. "A friend loves at all times, and a brother is born for a time of adversity" (17:17).

At all times. Not when it's convenient. Not when you're fun to be around. Not when there's something in it for them. A real friend loves when you're struggling, when you've failed, when everyone else has walked away. That kind of loyalty is rare, and Proverbs treats it as one of the most valuable things in the world.

The next verse adds an important dimension: "There is a friend who sticks closer than a brother" (18:24). In the ancient world, family bonds were the strongest ties anyone had. To say that a friend could be closer than a brother was a stunning claim. It meant that friendship, at its best, wasn't a lesser version of family. It was its own kind of bond, chosen freely and maintained through loyalty, trust, and mutual commitment.

But Proverbs is honest about the fact that not all friendships survive hard times. "Wealth attracts many friends, but even the closest friend of the poor person deserts them" (19:4). When things are going well, everyone wants to be around you. When things fall apart, you find out who your real friends are. Prosperity attracts company; adversity reveals character.

This is a proverb that almost everyone understands instinctively, even if they've never read the Bible. You already know what it feels like when someone is your best friend on Monday and ignores you on Tuesday because a more popular option came along. Proverbs doesn't pretend that doesn't happen. It tells you the truth about it so you can learn to value the friends who stay.

WHAT DESTROYS A FRIENDSHIP

If Proverbs tells you what builds a friendship, it also tells you what tears one apart. "A perverse person stirs up conflict, and a gossip separates close friends" (16:28).

There it is again: gossip. We covered this in the last chapter, but here it shows up with a specific target. Gossip doesn't just damage individuals. It destroys friendships. It takes two people who trust each other and drives a wedge between them with whispered stories, half-truths, and "Did you hear what they said about you?"

"Whoever would foster love covers over an offense, but whoever repeats the matter separates close friends" (17:9). This is one of the wisest verses in the entire book. Love lets things go. Love doesn't keep a record of every offense and pull it out during the next argument. Love gives the benefit of the doubt and moves on. But the person who keeps bringing up old failures, who won't let a mistake die, who repeats the story to others, that person is tearing the friendship apart with their own hands.

Think about your own friendships. Have you ever had a friend who wouldn't let something go? Who kept bringing up the same incident, the same mistake, the same argument, long after it should have been over? It's exhausting. It erodes trust. And eventually, it kills the relationship entirely.

Proverbs says: if you want to keep your friends, learn to forgive. And once you've forgiven, stop repeating the offense. To yourself, and especially to others.

YOU CAN'T WALK TWO PATHS

Here's the thing Proverbs keeps circling back to: you have to choose. You cannot walk with the wise and hang out with fools at the same time. You cannot sharpen your character with one group and dull it with another. The two paths diverge, and you have to pick one. "The righteous choose their friends carefully, but the way of the wicked leads them astray" (12:26).

That word "carefully" matters. Friendship isn't something that should just happen to you. It's something you should think about, pray about, and choose with intention. Who are you spending your time with? Are they making you wiser or more foolish? Are they sharpening you or wearing you down? Are they the kind of people who will tell you the truth when it hurts, or the kind who will flatter you all the way to disaster?

You don't need a hundred friends. You need a few who are walking the right direction and willing to take you with them.

"Plans fail for lack of counsel, but with many advisers they succeed" (15:22). The wise person doesn't try to figure out life alone. They surround themselves with people who can offer perspective, correction, and guidance. They build a circle of friends who function like a team, each one contributing something the others lack.

That's what the book of Proverbs envisions when it talks about friendship. Not just people to hang out with. Not just people who make you feel good. People who make you better. People who love you enough to tell you the truth, stand with you in hard times, and push you toward the life God designed you to live.

WHAT THIS MEANS FOR US

First, your friends are shaping you whether you realize it or not. You become like the people you spend the most time with. This isn't just a proverb. It's a law of human nature. If you want to know where your life is heading, look at the five people you spend the most time with. Their direction is probably yours.

Second, real friendship requires honesty, not just affirmation. The culture around you will tell you that a good friend is someone who always agrees with you, always supports your decisions, and never makes you uncomfortable. Proverbs says that's actually a description of a useless friend, or worse, an enemy. Real friends sharpen you. That means friction. That means hard conversations. That means choosing someone's long-term good over their short-term comfort.

Third, be the kind of friend Proverbs describes. It's easy to read this chapter and think about what you need from others. But Proverbs is also asking: Are *you* the kind of friend who sharpens? Are you loyal in hard times? Do you cover offenses or repeat them? Do you tell the truth in love, or do you flatter to keep the peace? The best way to attract wise friends is to become a wise friend.

Fourth, some friendships need to end. This is hard to say, but Proverbs is clear: if someone is consistently pulling you away from wisdom, if their influence is making you a worse person, if every time you're around them you find yourself compromising things you know are right, that's not a friendship worth keeping. Loyalty is a virtue, but loyalty to someone who is destroying you is not wisdom. It's a trap.

TALKING POINTS

1. **"Walk with the wise and become wise, for a companion of fools suffers harm" (13:20). Think about the people you spend the most time with.** In what ways are they shaping who you're becoming? Are there friendships in your life that are making you wiser? Are there any that might be pulling you in the wrong direction?

2. **"Iron sharpens iron, so one person sharpens another" (27:17). Sharpening involves friction, not just comfort.** When has a friend challenged you or told you something hard that ended up helping you? Why is that kind of honesty so rare, and how can you become better at both giving and receiving it?

3. **Proverbs warns against making friends with hot-tempered people because "you may learn their ways" (22:24–25).** What other negative traits do you think are contagious in friendships? How can you protect yourself from picking up bad habits from the people around you without completely isolating yourself?

4. **"Whoever would foster love covers over an offense, but whoever repeats the matter separates close friends" (17:9). Think of a time when holding onto a grudge damaged a relationship.** What does it look like to genuinely let something go? What's the difference between covering an offense in love and just pretending it didn't happen?

5. **Proverbs says "wealth attracts many friends, but even the closest friend of the poor person deserts them" (19:4).** Why do you think people are drawn to those who have something to offer them? How can you tell the difference between friends who are there for you and friends who are there for what you can give them?

Proverbs has shown you what real friendship looks like: iron that sharpens, love that endures, honesty that wounds in order to heal. It has also shown you the counterfeits: flattery that feels good but goes nowhere, company that entertains but corrupts, loyalty that lasts only as long as things are easy. The people you choose to walk with will shape the person you become. Choose carefully. Your future self will thank you.

Turn the page.

5

GET OFF THE COUCH

Mark Twain's *The Adventures of Tom Sawyer* has one of the most famous scenes in all of American literature. Tom has been ordered to whitewash a fence as punishment, and the thought of spending his Saturday doing manual labor while his friends play is almost more than he can bear. So he does what Tom Sawyer does best: he finds a way around it.

When his friend Ben walks by and starts mocking him, Tom pretends to be deeply absorbed in his work, as if painting a fence is the most fascinating activity in the world. "Does a boy get a chance to whitewash a fence every day?" he says. Before long, Ben is begging to take a turn, and Tom reluctantly "lets" him, but only in exchange for an apple. By the end of the afternoon, a parade of boys has come through, each one paying Tom for the privilege of doing his chore. Tom sits in the shade with a pile of treasures while the fence gets three coats of paint.

It's a funny scene. Tom is clever, charming, and resourceful. But here's the thing Twain understood and wrote into the story: Tom's cleverness is a particular kind of foolishness. He spends more energy avoiding work than the work itself would have required. He tricks others into laboring on his behalf while he contributes nothing. And the "wealth" he accumulates has no real value. It's a pile of junk: a dead rat on a string, twelve marbles, a piece of blue bottle glass, and a dog collar with no dog.

The book of Proverbs would look at Tom Sawyer and see a sluggard dressed up as an entrepreneur. And Proverbs has a lot to say about sluggards.

THE FUNNIEST VERSES IN THE BIBLE

Proverbs takes laziness seriously, but that doesn't mean it takes lazy people seriously. Some of the sharpest humor in all of Scripture is aimed squarely at the sluggard, and the portrait Proverbs paints is devastating precisely because it's so funny.

"The sluggard says, 'There's a lion outside! I'll be killed in the public square!'" (26:13). Imagine calling in sick to school because you heard there might be a lion in the parking lot. That's the sluggard's excuse. It's absurd, and it's meant to be. The lazy person always has a reason not to work, and the reason is always just plausible enough to sound legitimate while being completely ridiculous.

It gets better.

"As a door turns on its hinges, so a sluggard turns on his bed" (26:14). A door swings back and forth but never actually goes anywhere. That's the sluggard. Movement without progress. Rolling over, adjusting the pillow, checking the time, telling yourself "five more minutes" for the third time. You're moving, but you're not getting up.

"A sluggard buries his hand in the dish; he is too lazy to bring it back to his mouth" (26:15). This one is almost cartoonish. The lazy person has food right in front of him. All he has to do is lift it to his mouth. But even that feels like too much effort. The image is exaggerated on purpose. Proverbs is making a point through comedy: laziness, taken to its logical conclusion, is self-destruction disguised as comfort.

And then the final punch: "A sluggard is wiser in his own eyes than seven people who answer discreetly" (26:16). This might be the most cutting verse of the four. The sluggard doesn't just refuse to work. He thinks he's smarter than everyone who does. He's not lazy in his own mind. He's a "realist." He's not avoiding work. He's "working smarter, not harder." He has a reason for everything, and no amount of good advice from wise people can change his mind, because he already knows best.

One scholar described it perfectly: the sluggard has no idea he's lazy. He's not a shirker but a "realist." He's not self-indulgent but "below his best in the morning." His inertia is "an objection to being hustled." His mental laziness is simply "sticking to his guns."

Sound like anyone you know? Proverbs hopes it sounds like you, at least enough to make you uncomfortable.

GO WATCH THE ANTS

If the sluggard passages are the funniest part of Proverbs, the ant passage might be the most humbling.

"Go to the ant, you sluggard; consider its ways and be wise! It has no commander, no overseer or ruler, yet it stores its provisions in summer and gathers its food at harvest" (6:6–8).

The ant has no boss. Nobody makes it work. Nobody stands over it with a clipboard checking off tasks. It works because the work needs to be done, and it has the sense to do it at the right time. It doesn't wait until winter to start gathering food. It works in summer, when the opportunity is right, because it understands something the sluggard doesn't: the right time to prepare for tomorrow is today.

Then comes the warning: "How long will you lie there, you sluggard? When will you get up from your sleep? A little sleep, a little slumber, a little folding of the hands to rest, and poverty will come on you like a thief and scarcity like an armed man" (6:9–11).

Notice the word "little." The sluggard doesn't think he's being lazy. He's just resting a little bit. Just a few more minutes. Just this one more episode. Just one more scroll through the phone. Each individual choice seems tiny. But small surrenders add up. Poverty doesn't usually arrive all at once. It creeps in while you're folding your hands.

This is the pattern Proverbs keeps highlighting: laziness isn't one dramatic decision. It's a thousand small ones. It's the student who doesn't study tonight because the test is next week, and then doesn't study tomorrow because there's still time, and then panics the night before because the time is gone. It's the slow erosion of opportunity through a series of "not right now" decisions that eventually become "too late."

WHY WORK MATTERS

Proverbs doesn't just mock the lazy. It celebrates the diligent.

"All hard work brings a profit, but mere talk leads only to poverty" (14:23). There's a directness to that sentence that's hard to argue with. Talk is cheap. Plans without execution are worthless. But actual effort, even imperfect effort, produces something. The person who shows up and does the work, day after day, will build something over time. The person who only talks about what they're going to do someday will have nothing to show for it.

"Diligent hands will rule, but laziness ends in forced labor" (12:24). The irony is sharp. The lazy person avoids work because they want freedom, but their laziness eventually takes their freedom away. The diligent person accepts the discipline of work and ends up in a position of authority and influence. Proverbs sees this as a basic law of how the world operates.

"Those who work their land will have abundant food, but those who chase fantasies have no sense" (12:11). The phrase "chase fantasies" is worth lingering on. It's the ancient version of get-rich-quick schemes, viral fame overnight, or the idea that you can skip the hard part and jump straight to success. Proverbs says that's not how reality works. There are no shortcuts that bypass effort. The person who puts in the daily, unglamorous work of tending their field will eat. The person who chases fantasies will go hungry.

This isn't a message our culture loves to hear. We celebrate the overnight success, the viral moment, the shortcut to wealth. But Proverbs insists that lasting prosperity is built slowly, through consistent effort over time. "Dishonest money dwindles away, but whoever gathers money little by little makes it grow" (13:11). Little by little. Not all at once. Not through a clever scheme. Through patient, steady, faithful work.

MONEY ISN'T WHAT YOU THINK IT IS

If Proverbs values hard work, you might expect it to treat wealth as the ultimate reward. It doesn't. In fact, some of the most surprising verses in the book are the ones that put money in its place.

"Better a little with the fear of the Lord than great wealth with turmoil" (15:16).

"Better a little with righteousness than much gain with injustice" (16:8).

"A good name is more desirable than great riches; to be esteemed is better than silver or gold" (22:1).

Read those carefully. Proverbs isn't saying money is evil. It's saying money is not the most important thing. If you have to choose between wealth and a right relationship with God, choose God. If you have to choose between getting rich and keeping your integrity, keep your integrity. If you have to choose between a fat bank account and a good reputation, take the reputation every time.

This is where Proverbs gets genuinely countercultural. Our world measures success almost entirely by money. How much do you make? What do you own? What can you afford? Proverbs says those are the wrong questions. The right question is: What kind of person are you becoming while you earn it?

"Do not wear yourself out to get rich; do not trust your own cleverness. Cast but a glance at riches, and they are gone, for they will surely sprout wings and fly off to the sky like an eagle" (23:4–5). Money is temporary. It disappears. It's here today and gone tomorrow, no matter how tightly you grip it. Building your life around accumulating money is like building a house on a foundation that keeps shifting.

And then there's this remarkable prayer from a man named Agur, near the end of the book: "Give me neither poverty nor riches, but give me only my daily bread. Otherwise, I may have too much and disown you and say, 'Who is the Lord?' Or I may become poor and steal, and so dishonor the name of my God" (30:8–9).

That prayer is stunning in its honesty. Agur isn't asking for wealth. He isn't romanticizing poverty either. He's asking for just enough, because he understands that both extremes are spiritually dangerous. Too much money tempts you to forget God. Too little tempts you to compromise your integrity. The sweet spot is somewhere in the middle, where you have what you need and your dependence on God stays intact.

THE GENEROSITY TEST

Proverbs doesn't just tell you how to earn money wisely. It tells you how to spend it wisely. And the clearest test of whether you've understood what Proverbs teaches about wealth is this: are you generous?

"One person gives freely, yet gains even more; another withholds unduly, but comes to poverty" (11:24). That's a paradox, and it's meant to be. Common sense says that giving away money makes you poorer. Proverbs says the opposite is true. Generosity opens doors that hoarding closes. The person who shares what they have, who sees the needs of others and responds, who doesn't clutch their resources with a white-knuckle grip, that person will somehow end up with more, not less.

"Whoever is kind to the poor lends to the Lord, and he will reward them for what they have done" (19:17). Think about that image. When you give to someone in need, God considers it a personal loan to himself. He takes it that seriously. And he promises to pay it back.

"Those who give to the poor will lack nothing, but those who close their eyes to them receive many curses" (28:27). Proverbs is remarkably consistent on this point. Generosity toward the vulnerable isn't optional. It's not something you do after you've taken care of yourself. It's a core feature of how the wise person lives.

And Proverbs reminds you why. "Rich and poor have this in common: the Lord is the Maker of them all" (22:2). The person who has nothing and the person who has everything were both made by the same God. Neither one is more valuable than the other. When you close your eyes to someone in need, you're closing your eyes to someone God made and God loves.

WHAT THIS MEANS FOR US

First, laziness is more dangerous than it looks. It doesn't announce itself as laziness. It disguises itself as rest, as waiting for the right moment, as being "realistic." But the sluggard's small surrenders add up to big losses. The ant doesn't need a boss to get moving. Neither should you. Whatever is in front of you to do, do it now, and do it well.

Second, work is a gift, not a curse. Proverbs never describes work as something to be avoided or endured. It describes work as the normal, healthy way that wise people build their lives. Hard work brings a profit. Diligent hands gain influence. The person who tends their field eats. Don't resent the effort. Lean into it.

Third, money makes a terrible god. Wealth is useful. Proverbs doesn't deny that. But wealth is not the measure of your life, and pursuing it at the expense of your character, your relationships, or your faith is the definition of foolishness. The best things in life, Proverbs says over and over, cannot be bought.

Fourth, generosity is the true test of wisdom. It's easy to say you trust God when your bank account is full. Generosity proves it. When you give to those who can't repay you, when you share what you have instead of hoarding it, when you see a need and respond, you're living out what Proverbs teaches about how the world is supposed to work.

Fifth, pray Agur's prayer. "Give me neither poverty nor riches." That's the prayer of a person who understands both the danger of having too little and the danger of having too much. It's the prayer of someone who wants just enough to live faithfully, with both hands open instead of clenched.

TALKING POINTS

1. **The sluggard in Proverbs 26:13–16 always has an excuse and is "wiser in his own eyes" than everyone else.** Why do you think lazy people rarely see themselves as lazy? What excuses do you catch yourself making when you don't want to do something?

2. **The ant works without a boss, without anyone forcing it to prepare for the future.** What areas of your life require you to work without someone standing over you? What helps you stay motivated when no one is watching?

3. **Proverbs says "a good name is more desirable than great riches" (22:1).** In a world that constantly measures success by

money, what does it look like to value your reputation and character more than wealth? Can you think of someone whose good name is clearly more valuable to them than money?

4. **Agur prayed for "neither poverty nor riches" because both extremes are spiritually dangerous.** Do you agree? Why would having too much money be dangerous? Have you ever seen wealth change someone's relationship with God?

5. **Proverbs says those who give freely "gain even more" (11:24).** Why do you think generosity leads to abundance instead of scarcity? What's one practical way you could be more generous this week with what you have, whether that's money, time, or something else?

Proverbs has taken you from the lunch table to the ant hill, from the sluggard's bed to Agur's prayer. The message weaving through it all is simple but relentless: how you work and how you handle money reveals what you really believe about God. The lazy person trusts only in comfort. The greedy person trusts only in wealth. The wise person works hard, holds possessions loosely, gives freely, and trusts that the God who made everything will provide what is needed.

Turn the page.

6

THE WAR INSIDE

Inside Out 2 picks up where the original left off, but with a twist that anyone in their teenage years will recognize instantly. Riley is thirteen now, heading to hockey camp, trying to impress the older girls, and desperate to fit in. Joy, Sadness, Anger, Fear, and Disgust are still running the control panel inside her head. But then, without warning, new emotions show up. Anxiety barges in and starts rearranging everything. Envy quietly takes a seat and starts comparing Riley to everyone around her. Embarrassment hides in the corner, enormous and self-conscious.

What makes the movie so effective is the moment Anxiety takes over the console. She doesn't do it out of malice. She genuinely believes she's protecting Riley. But her version of protection is control, and her control slowly rewrites Riley's entire sense of who she is. The beliefs that Joy carefully built over the years get boxed up and replaced with Anxiety's version: "I'm not good enough. I need to be someone else to be accepted. If I don't perform perfectly, everything will fall apart."

By the end of the movie, Riley learns that no single emotion gets to run the show. Her identity isn't determined by whichever feeling screams the loudest. She has to learn to let all her emotions exist without letting any one of them take over.

That's a pretty good summary of what Proverbs teaches about character. The book of Proverbs is deeply interested in what's happening inside you. Not just your actions, but the internal forces that drive them. Pride, humility, anger, patience, envy, self-control, teachability: these are the battlegrounds where your character is formed. And according to Proverbs, the war you fight inside yourself matters more than any battle you fight in the world around you.

THE MONSTER CALLED PRIDE

If Proverbs has a number one enemy, it's pride.

"Pride goes before destruction, a haughty spirit before a fall" (16:18). That sentence is so famous it's become a common English expression. But most people quote it wrong. They say "pride goes before a fall," as if it's just about embarrassing yourself after bragging too much. Proverbs means something much bigger. The word "destruction" isn't a stumble. It's a collapse. Pride doesn't just trip you up. It takes you down.

Why is pride so dangerous? Because it blocks the one thing you need most: the ability to learn. A proud person already knows everything, or thinks they do. A proud person doesn't listen to advice, doesn't accept correction, and doesn't admit when they're wrong. Proverbs describes this person with one of its sharpest images: "Do you see a person wise in their own eyes? There is more hope for a fool than for them" (26:12).

Let that sink in. Throughout the entire book, the fool is the lowest category of person. The fool rejects wisdom, mocks instruction, and heads straight for disaster. And yet Proverbs says there is more hope for a fool than for someone who is convinced they already have it all figured out. Why? Because the fool might eventually realize they need help. The person who is wise in their own eyes never will.

"When pride comes, then comes disgrace, but with humility comes wisdom" (11:2). Pride and wisdom cannot live in the same house. If you're full of yourself, there's no room left for wisdom to enter. But humility opens the door. Humility says, "I might be wrong. I don't know everything. I need to listen." And that posture is the only one in which wisdom can grow.

"Before a downfall the heart is haughty, but humility comes before honor" (18:12). Notice the order. The haughty heart comes *before* the fall. You don't become proud after succeeding; the pride was already there, quietly setting you up for failure. In the same way, humility comes *before* honor. You don't humble yourself after you've been honored. The humility was what put you in a position to receive honor in the first place.

Proverbs is telling you something important about cause and effect: the thing happening inside you right now is determining what happens to you next. Your internal posture sets the direction of your external life.

ANGER AND THE PATIENT PERSON

If pride is Proverbs' number one enemy, uncontrolled anger might be number two.

"A quick-tempered person does foolish things" (14:17). There's no ambiguity there. Quick anger leads to foolish actions. Every single time? Proverbs would say: often enough that you should take it very seriously. The person who flies off the handle doesn't think clearly, doesn't weigh consequences, and ends up doing things they'll regret as soon as the heat passes.

"Fools give full vent to their rage, but the wise bring calm in the end" (29:11). "Full vent" is the key phrase. The fool holds nothing back. Whatever they feel, they blast it out, unfiltered, at full volume. The wise person, by contrast, brings calm. Not because they never feel anger, but because they've learned to manage what they feel instead of being managed by it.

"A hot-tempered person stirs up conflict, but the one who is patient calms a quarrel" (15:18). Proverbs sees this as a straightforward observation about how life works. Hotheads create problems. Patient people solve them. If you want to know which kind of person you're becoming, look at what happens to the emotional temperature of a room when you walk in. Do things get calmer? Or do they get more volatile?

And then comes one of the most striking comparisons in the entire book: "Better a patient person than a warrior, one with self-control than one who takes a city" (16:32). Read that again. In the ancient world, conquering a city was the ultimate achievement. Generals were celebrated for it. Kings built their legacies on it. And Proverbs says that a person who can control their own temper has accomplished something greater. Taking a city requires strength, strategy, and courage. Controlling yourself when every nerve in your body wants to explode requires something deeper.

This is the kind of strength that doesn't make headlines. Nobody gives you a trophy for not sending the angry text. Nobody applauds when you walk away from a fight instead of escalating it. But Proverbs says that kind of self-mastery is more impressive than military conquest. And it's right.

A CITY WITH BROKEN WALLS

Proverbs uses a vivid image for what happens when self-control breaks down: "Like a city whose walls are broken through is a person who lacks self-control" (25:28).

In the ancient world, a city's walls were its primary defense. Without walls, a city was exposed to every enemy, every raider, every threat. The walls didn't just keep bad things out. They defined the city itself. A city without walls was barely a city at all.

That's what you're like without self-control. You're exposed. Every temptation walks right in. Every impulse gets acted on. Every emotion runs the show. You have no defense against the things that want to take you apart, because you've torn down the walls yourself.

Self-control, in Proverbs, isn't about suppressing who you are. It's about protecting who you are. The walls don't make the city a prison. They make it a city. In the same way, self-control doesn't make you less free. It makes you the kind of person who can actually choose their actions instead of being dragged around by whatever feeling happens to be strongest at the moment.

THE ROT OF ENVY

Proverbs doesn't say as much about envy as it does about pride or anger, but what it does say is striking.

"A heart at peace gives life to the body, but envy rots the bones" (14:30). The image is almost medical. A peaceful heart produces health. Envy produces decay, not on the surface where people can see it, but deep in the bones, in the structure that holds everything together. Envy eats you from the inside out.

Think about what envy actually does to you. When you envy someone, you can't enjoy what you have because you're too busy resenting what they have. Their success feels like your failure. Their happiness feels like an insult. You spend your emotional energy measuring yourself against someone else's life instead of building your own.

"Do not let your heart envy sinners, but always be zealous for the fear of the Lord" (23:17). This verse adds an important dimension. Sometimes the people you envy aren't even people worth imitating. They might have things you want, but they got those things through shortcuts, dishonesty, or selfishness. Envying them means wanting to be like them, and that's the last thing you should want. The antidote to envy isn't getting what they have. It's redirecting your heart toward what actually matters: the fear of the Lord, which is where all wisdom begins.

"Do not fret because of evildoers or be envious of the wicked, for the evildoer has no future hope, and the lamp of the wicked will be snuffed out" (24:19–20). Envy assumes that someone else's situation is permanent and that yours is too. Proverbs says neither is true. The wicked may look like they're winning right now, but their prosperity has an expiration date. Don't compare your middle to someone else's highlight reel. Their story isn't over, and neither is yours.

THE TEACHABLE SPIRIT

The flip side of pride is teachability, and Proverbs values it above almost everything else.

"Whoever loves discipline loves knowledge, but whoever hates correction is stupid" (12:1). That last word is intentionally blunt. The person who refuses to be corrected isn't just unwise. They're acting like an animal that can't reason. They've shut down the very faculty that makes growth possible.

"The way of fools seems right to them, but the wise listen to advice" (12:15). Here's the telltale sign. Fools are absolutely certain they're on the right path. They don't need input. They don't need a second opinion. They've already decided. And that certainty is exactly what makes them fools. The wise, on the other hand, have learned that their own perspective is limited and that other people can see things they can't.

"Rebuke the wise and they will love you. Instruct the wise and they will be wiser still" (9:8–9). This is a remarkable test of character. How do you respond when someone corrects you? If your first reaction is defensiveness, if you immediately look for reasons the criticism is wrong, if you feel attacked, those reactions reveal something about the condition of your heart. But if you can hear a rebuke and think, "They might be right. Let me consider this," you're displaying one of the rarest and most valuable traits a person can have.

"Listen to advice and accept discipline, and at the end you will be counted among the wise" (19:20). Notice the phrase "at the end." Wisdom isn't instant. It's the result of a long process of listening, being corrected, adjusting, and listening again. Nobody becomes wise in a day. But the person who maintains a teachable spirit over time will get there. The one who resists correction never will.

"A rebuke impresses a discerning person more than a hundred lashes a fool" (17:10). The wise person needs only a word. A single correction, delivered honestly, goes deep and produces change. The fool, by contrast, can't be reached even by extreme consequences. They bounce off. They don't penetrate. The difference isn't intelligence. It's openness.

WHAT THIS MEANS FOR US

First, the war inside you is the war that matters most. Proverbs doesn't spend most of its time talking about external enemies. It talks about pride, anger, envy, and the refusal to learn, because those are the forces that actually destroy people from within. You can succeed at everything the world measures and still be falling apart inside. The internal battles are the ones that shape your character, and character determines your destiny.

Second, pride is the root of almost every other failure. When you're too proud to listen, you miss the correction that could save you. When you're too proud to apologize, you lose relationships that matter. When you're too proud to admit you're wrong, you keep walking the wrong direction. Humility isn't weakness. It's the foundation that everything else is built on.

Third, self-control is the wall that protects everything else. Without it, every good quality you have is vulnerable. You can be intelligent, talented, and well-intentioned, but if you can't control your temper, your impulses, or your reactions, those qualities won't save you. Building self-control is one of the most important things you can do at any age, but especially now, while your habits are still forming.

Fourth, envy is a thief that steals your peace. It takes what should be contentment and replaces it with constant comparison. The cure is gratitude and a redirected heart. Instead of looking sideways at what someone else has, look upward at what God has given you and forward at what he's building in you.

Fifth, make teachability your lifelong goal. The smartest people you'll ever meet are the ones who still think they have something to learn. The most dangerous people are the ones who stopped listening years ago. Every correction you receive with grace makes you a little wiser. Every correction you reject with defensiveness makes you a little more foolish.

TALKING POINTS

1. **"Pride goes before destruction, a haughty spirit before a fall" (16:18).** Why do you think pride is so dangerous? Can you think of a time when overconfidence led to a mistake in your own life or in someone else's?

2. **Proverbs says a patient person is "better than a warrior" and that self-control is greater than "taking a city" (16:32).** Why do you think controlling yourself is considered a greater achievement than controlling others? What makes self-control so difficult?

3. **"A heart at peace gives life to the body, but envy rots the bones" (14:30).** What does envy feel like when it starts? How does it affect the way you see yourself and the people around you? What helps you fight it?

4. **"The way of fools seems right to them, but the wise listen to advice" (12:15).** How can you tell the difference between healthy confidence and being "wise in your own eyes"? What makes it hard to accept correction, even when you know the person correcting you is right?

5. **"Like a city whose walls are broken through is a person who lacks self-control" (25:28).** What are the "walls" in your life that protect you from making bad decisions? What habits or practices help you maintain self-control when your emotions are running high?

The battles that matter most don't happen where anyone can see them. They happen in the silence of your own heart, in the split second between feeling an impulse and choosing whether to follow it. Pride whispers that you don't need anyone's help. Anger demands that you react right now. Envy says you'll never have enough. And the quiet voice of wisdom says: slow down, listen, stay humble, and trust that the God who made you knows what he's doing.

That voice doesn't scream. But it's the only one worth following.

Turn the page.

7

DO WHAT'S RIGHT

Picture this. You're at the register paying for something, and the cashier hands you back your change. You shove it in your pocket and walk out. A few minutes later, you count the money and realize she gave you ten dollars too much. Nobody saw. Nobody will ever know. The cashier probably won't notice until the drawer comes up short at the end of the shift, and even then she won't know who got the extra cash. You could keep it and nothing would happen to you.

So what do you do?

Most people, if they're being honest, would admit that the temptation to keep it is real. It's not like you stole anything. *She* made the mistake. And it's only ten dollars. But somewhere in the back of your mind, a quieter voice asks: What kind of person do I want to be? Not "What can I get away with?" but "Who am I when nobody's looking?"

That question is at the heart of everything Proverbs teaches about justice and integrity. Because Proverbs isn't ultimately interested in whether you follow the rules when someone is checking. It's interested in what you do when no one is checking, because that's when your character is actually on display.

And here's the part that might surprise you: Proverbs says that even when no one else is watching, someone is.

"The eyes of the Lord are everywhere, keeping watch on the wicked and the good" (15:3).

"A person may think their own ways are right, but the Lord weighs the heart" (21:2).

You can fool other people. You can sometimes fool yourself. But you can't fool God. He sees the extra ten dollars in your pocket. He sees the homework you copied. He sees the way you treated the kid nobody else pays attention to. He sees what you do in private, and according to Proverbs, he cares deeply about all of it.

HONEST SCALES

One of the most repeated themes in the entire book of Proverbs is God's hatred of dishonesty, and one of the most concrete ways it shows up is in the image of scales and weights.

"The Lord detests dishonest scales, but accurate weights find his favor" (11:1).

"Honest scales and balances belong to the Lord; all the weights in the bag are of his making" (16:11).

"Differing weights and differing measures, the Lord detests them both" (20:10).

In the ancient world, buying and selling was done by weighing goods on a balance. A merchant could cheat a customer by using rigged weights, making an item seem heavier or lighter than it really was. The customer wouldn't know. The scales looked fine. The transaction appeared legitimate. But the weights were dishonest, and the merchant pocketed the difference.

Proverbs says God detests this. Not "disapproves." Not "frowns upon." *Detests.* That's one of the strongest words in the entire Old Testament for divine anger. The God who created the universe has a visceral reaction to dishonesty in everyday transactions.

You probably don't use scales to buy grain at the market. But the principle translates perfectly into your life. Dishonest scales are any situation where you present something as fair when it isn't. Copying someone's homework and putting your name on it. Taking credit for work you didn't do. Telling a half-truth that technically isn't a lie but is designed to mislead. Manipulating a situation so that it benefits you at someone else's expense.

Every one of those is a rigged scale. And God sees every one of them.

But the flip side is equally important: "accurate weights find his favor." Honesty pleases God. When you tell the truth even though a lie would be easier, when you give credit where it's due, when you play fair even when cheating would go unnoticed, something happens that you can't see but that Proverbs insists is real. You gain God's favor. The Creator of the universe looks at your small act of integrity and is pleased.

THE KIND OF PERSON GOD DELIGHTS IN

Proverbs draws a clear line between what God loves and what he hates. And when you lay the two lists side by side, a portrait emerges of the kind of person God is looking for.

"The Lord detests lying lips, but he delights in people who are trustworthy" (12:22).

"To do what is right and just is more acceptable to the Lord than sacrifice" (21:3).

That second verse is remarkable. In ancient Israel, sacrifice was the centerpiece of worship. It was the most visible, most formal way of honoring God. And Proverbs says that doing what is right and just matters more. You can go through all the motions of religion, attend every service, say all the right prayers, but if your daily life doesn't reflect justice and integrity, God is not impressed.

"The integrity of the upright guides them, but the unfaithful are destroyed by their duplicity" (11:3). Integrity isn't just a nice quality. It's a guide. When you're honest at your core, decision-making becomes simpler. You don't have to remember which story you told to which person. You don't have to cover your tracks. You don't have to worry about being found out. You just tell the truth and let the chips fall where they may. Integrity simplifies your life. Duplicity complicates it, and eventually it collapses under its own weight.

"Whoever walks in integrity walks securely, but whoever takes crooked paths will be found out" (10:9). There's a confidence that comes with honesty. You can look people in the eye because you have nothing to hide. But the person who lives deceptively is always looking over their shoulder, always managing their story, always one conversation away from being exposed. Proverbs says the exposure is inevitable. It's not a question of if but when.

GOD AND THE VULNERABLE

If Proverbs cares about honesty in everyday transactions, it cares even more about how the powerful treat the powerless. And on this topic, Proverbs doesn't just offer suggestions. It delivers warnings.

"Whoever oppresses the poor shows contempt for their Maker, but whoever is kind to the needy honors God" (14:31). Read that slowly. When you mistreat someone who is vulnerable, you aren't just being cruel to them. You are showing contempt for God, because God made that person. They bear his image. They matter to him. To treat them as if they don't matter is to tell God that his creation is worthless.

"Whoever mocks the poor shows contempt for their Maker" (17:5). It's not just active oppression that Proverbs condemns. It's mockery. It's the casual cruelty of laughing at someone who has less than you, making fun of someone's clothes, or treating someone as invisible because they can't do anything for you. Proverbs says God takes that personally.

"Do not exploit the poor because they are poor and do not crush the needy in court, for the Lord will take up their case and will exact life for life" (22:22–23). This is not a gentle warning. God will *take up their case*. He will act as their lawyer, their defender, their advocate. And the punishment for those who exploit the vulnerable won't be a slap on the wrist. Proverbs says God will "exact life for life." The stakes are that high.

"Whoever shuts their ears to the cry of the poor will also cry out and not be answered" (21:13). This one cuts deep. If you ignore people who need help, the day will come when you need help, and no one will answer. The principle is reciprocal. How you treat the vulnerable is how you will eventually be treated.

And then there's this, one of the most direct commands in the entire book: "Speak up for those who cannot speak for themselves, for the rights of all who are destitute. Speak up and judge fairly; defend the rights of the poor and needy" (31:8–9).

These words were originally directed at a king, but the principle applies to everyone. When you see someone being treated unfairly, when you see someone who can't defend themselves, when you see injustice happening and you have the ability to say something, Proverbs says: open your mouth. Don't stay silent because it's easier. Don't look the other way because it's not your problem. The wise person uses their voice for the voiceless.

WHY IT MATTERS WHEN NO ONE IS WATCHING

Everything in this chapter circles back to a single idea: your character is defined not by what you do on stage but by what you do backstage.

"Even small children are known by their actions, by whether their conduct is pure and right" (20:11). You're not too young for your actions to reveal your character. Every choice you make, every day, in situations no one else sees, is building the person you're becoming. The question isn't whether anyone notices right now. The question is what kind of person you're assembling, choice by choice, when the spotlight is off.

"For your ways are in full view of the Lord, and he examines all your paths" (5:21). This isn't meant to make you paranoid. It's meant to give you perspective. You're never actually alone. The God who sees everything isn't watching to catch you messing up. He's watching because he cares about what you're becoming. And he wants you to become the kind of person who does the right thing, not because someone is checking, but because it's right.

"The righteous lead blameless lives; blessed are their children after them" (20:7). Integrity isn't just about you. It ripples outward. The people around you, especially the ones watching you most closely, are affected by the character you build. Your future family, your future friends, your future community will all be shaped by whether you chose integrity or took shortcuts.

"Acquitting the guilty and condemning the innocent, the Lord detests them both" (17:15). God hates injustice in every direction. He hates it when guilty people escape consequences, and he hates it when innocent people get blamed for things they didn't do. If you've ever been falsely accused, you know how that feels. Proverbs says God knows too, and he cares.

WHAT THIS MEANS FOR US

First, integrity is who you are when no one is looking. It's easy to be honest when people are watching, when there are consequences for getting caught, when your reputation is on the line. The real test is what you do when you could get away with it. That's when your character speaks loudest.

Second, God sees everything, and that should be a comfort, not a threat. The fact that God watches your paths means that your quiet acts of honesty and courage are never wasted. Nobody else may notice when you give back the extra change, stand up for the kid being picked on, or tell the truth when a lie would be easier. But God notices. And according to Proverbs, he delights in it.

Third, how you treat vulnerable people reveals who you really are. It's easy to be kind to people who can do something for you. Proverbs measures your character by how you treat people who can't. The kid who eats alone. The person everyone ignores. The one who can't fight back. How you treat them is how you treat God.

Fourth, speak up. One of the hardest forms of integrity is using your voice when it would be safer to stay quiet. When you see someone being treated unfairly, when you know the truth and everyone else is going along with a lie, when someone who can't defend themselves needs an advocate, wisdom says: say something. Silence in the face of injustice is not neutrality. It's a choice.

Fifth, small choices build big character. You don't become a person of integrity through one dramatic moment. You become one through a thousand small decisions: telling the truth about something minor, returning money that isn't yours, refusing to join in when the group turns against someone, doing the right thing when it costs you nothing except your convenience. Those small choices are the bricks that build the house of your character.

TALKING POINTS

1. **Proverbs says "the eyes of the Lord are everywhere" (15:3) and "he examines all your paths" (5:21).** Does knowing that God sees everything make you feel comforted or uncomfortable? Why? How should it change the way you live?

2. **God "detests dishonest scales" but delights in "accurate weights" (11:1).** What are some modern versions of dishonest scales in your daily life? Where are you tempted to present something as fair when it really isn't?

3. **"Whoever oppresses the poor shows contempt for their Maker" (14:31).** Why do you think God takes the treatment of vulnerable people so personally? How does knowing that every person is made by God change the way you think about people who have less than you?

4. **Proverbs 31:8–9 says to "speak up for those who cannot speak for themselves."** When have you seen someone being treated unfairly and stayed silent? What made it hard to speak up? What would it look like to use your voice for someone who needs it?

5. **"Whoever walks in integrity walks securely" (10:9).** What does it feel like to have nothing to hide? What does it feel like to be hiding something? How does integrity make life simpler, even when it's harder in the moment?

Proverbs began this book by telling you that the fear of the Lord is the beginning of wisdom. This chapter shows what that looks like when it touches the ground. It looks like honest scales and truthful lips. It looks like caring about the people everyone else overlooks. It looks like speaking up when silence would be easier. It looks like being the same person in private that you are in public, because the God who sees both is the same God who made you and loves you and is building you into something the world desperately needs.

Turn the page.

8

QUESTIONS AND CHARACTER

Have you ever been in a class where the teacher finishes explaining something complicated and asks, "Does anyone have questions?" The room goes silent. Nobody raises a hand. Not because everyone understands, but because nobody wants to be the one who admits they're confused. The pressure to look like you've got it all figured out is enormous, especially when you're young. Asking a question feels like admitting you're behind. So you stay quiet, nod along, and hope you'll figure it out later.

Now imagine a man who is known for his wisdom. He's a respected sage, someone people listen to when he speaks. And the very first words out of his mouth are: "I am the most ignorant of men. I do not have a man's understanding. I have not learned wisdom, nor do I have knowledge of the Holy One" (30:2–3).

That's Agur, and he opens the second-to-last chapter of Proverbs by doing the one thing nobody in that silent classroom is willing to do. He raises his hand. He admits what he doesn't know. And by doing so, according to Proverbs, he takes the first and most important step toward actually becoming wise.

The final two chapters of Proverbs introduce us to two people most readers have never heard of: a man named Agur, who asks questions, and a woman described in a poem that has been read at dinner tables for thousands of years. Together, they bring the entire book to its conclusion and tie a bow on everything Proverbs has been teaching from the very beginning.

THE MAN WHO ADMITTED HE DIDN'T KNOW

Agur son of Jakeh is a mystery. He appears nowhere else in the Bible. Most scholars believe he was from Massa, an area in Arabia connected to the descendants of Ishmael. If that's right, he wasn't even an Israelite. He was an outsider whose words were considered wise enough to be included in Israel's sacred book.

And he starts by confessing his ignorance.

"I am too stupid to be a man; I do not have the understanding of a human being. I have not learned wisdom, nor do I have knowledge of the Holy One" (30:2–3).

Is he being literal? Probably not. One scholar called this "a frank confession of human frailty, ignorance, and uncertainty" that leads to "strong religious affirmation." Agur isn't dumb. He's doing something much harder than pretending to know everything. He's being honest about the limits of what any human being can figure out on their own.

Then he asks a series of breathtaking questions: "Who has gone up to heaven and come down? Who has gathered the wind in the hollow of his hands? Who has wrapped up the waters in his cloak? Who has established all the ends of the earth? What is his name, and the name of his son? Tell me if you know!" (30:4).

These questions echo the voice of God in the book of Job, where God challenges Job with similar questions about creation: "Where were you when I laid the earth's foundation?" (Job 38:4). The obvious answer to all of Agur's questions is: God. Only God has done these things. Only God has the comprehensive knowledge required to understand how the world really works.

And the point of asking questions you already know the answer to is this: if only God truly understands reality, then human beings need something beyond their own intelligence to live wisely. We need God's word. That's exactly where Agur goes next.

"Every word of God is flawless; he is a shield to those who take refuge in him. Do not add to his words, or he will rebuke you and prove you a liar" (30:5–6).

The logic is simple and powerful. We can't figure out life on our own. God can. He has spoken. His words are trustworthy. So the wise thing to do is to trust what he says rather than trusting our own limited understanding. Sound familiar? It's Proverbs 3:5–6 all over again: "Trust in the Lord with all your heart and lean not on your own understanding." Agur's humble questions lead him right back to the book's central message.

THE HONEST PRAYER

After his confession, Agur prays one of the most remarkable prayers in the Bible.

"Two things I ask of you, Lord; do not refuse me before I die: Keep falsehood and lies far from me; give me neither poverty nor riches, but give me only my daily bread. Otherwise,

I may have too much and disown you and say, 'Who is the Lord?' Or I may become poor and steal, and so dishonor the name of my God" (30:7–9).

We touched on this prayer in an earlier chapter, but it deserves another look here because of what it reveals about Agur's character. He doesn't pray for success, fame, wealth, or power. He prays for two things: honesty and just enough.

He wants to be a truthful person. And he wants the kind of life where he's neither so comfortable that he forgets God nor so desperate that he compromises his integrity. That's it. Those are his two requests. And the fact that he knows himself well enough to see both dangers tells you everything about why his words ended up in the Bible. Agur is the living example of what Proverbs has been teaching all along: humility, honesty, and a healthy fear of God are the marks of a truly wise person.

WONDER AT THE WORLD

The rest of chapter 30 shifts from confession and prayer to something unexpected: a series of observations about the natural world that read almost like a nature documentary narrated by a poet.

Agur is fascinated by what he sees around him. He groups things into patterns, using a distinctive "three things, even four" structure that invites the reader to look at familiar things with fresh eyes.

"There are four things on earth that are small, yet they are extremely wise: Ants are creatures of little strength, yet they store up their food in the summer; rock badgers are creatures of little power, yet they make their homes in the crags; locusts have no king, yet they advance together in ranks; a lizard can be caught with the hand, yet it is found in kings' palaces" (30:24–28).

These four tiny creatures each compensate for their weakness with a particular kind of wisdom. The ants plan ahead. The rock badgers find security outside themselves. The locusts work together without needing a boss. The lizard, small enough to catch in your hand, somehow ends up living in the most protected and prestigious place in the land.

Agur isn't giving a science lesson. He's holding up a mirror. If creatures this small and vulnerable can thrive by using the wisdom God gave them, what excuse does a human being have for refusing to do the same? The ants don't complain about being small. The rock badgers don't try to fight predators with muscle they don't have. They use what they've been given wisely, and they survive. The lesson is clear: wisdom isn't about being the strongest or the smartest. It's about knowing what you have, knowing what you don't, and acting accordingly.

This is the same man who opened the chapter by confessing his ignorance. And that's the connection. Agur's humility before God doesn't make him less observant about the world. It makes him more observant. Because when you stop pretending you know everything, you start actually seeing what's in front of you. Wonder is the reward of humility.

A MOTHER'S ADVICE TO A KING

Chapter 31 opens with a brief but important passage: the words of King Lemuel, which his mother taught him. Like Agur, Lemuel is probably from Massa, and his mother's advice is practical and direct.

She warns him against wasting his strength on things that destroy kings (31:3), tells him to stay sober so he can think clearly and judge fairly (31:4–5), and then gives him a command that echoes what we read in the previous chapter about justice:

"Speak up for those who cannot speak for themselves, for the rights of all who are destitute. Speak up and judge fairly; defend the rights of the poor and needy" (31:8–9).

A king's job, according to this mother, isn't to accumulate power for himself. It's to use his power for the powerless. This teaching fits hand in glove with everything Proverbs has already said about justice and caring for the vulnerable. But it's striking that these words come from a mother. Throughout the entire book, Proverbs has insisted that wisdom is taught by both father and mother (1:8). Here, at the very end, a mother gets the last word on what it means to lead well.

THE WOMAN WORTH KNOWING

And then comes the poem. Proverbs 31:10–31 is one of the most famous passages in the entire Old Testament. It's an acrostic poem, meaning each verse starts with the next letter of the Hebrew alphabet, from beginning to end. It's a complete portrait, A to Z, of a woman of extraordinary character.

"A wife of noble character, who can find? She is worth far more than rubies" (31:10).

What follows is a portrait of a woman who works tirelessly, manages her household with skill, conducts business with shrewdness, provides for her family, helps the poor, speaks with wisdom, and faces the future with confidence. She gets up before dawn and her lamp doesn't go out at night. She plants vineyards and makes clothes. She opens her arms to the poor and extends her hands to the needy. Her children rise up and bless her. Her husband praises her.

Now, here's where you need to read carefully, because this poem has been badly misused over the years. It has been turned into a checklist, as if the point is that every woman needs to wake up at 4 a.m., run a small business, sew her own clothes, and buy real estate, all before breakfast. That's not what this poem is doing.

This poem is a portrait of what wisdom looks like when it takes human form.

Remember what happened in chapter 9? Two women stood on the highest point of the city. Woman Wisdom built a magnificent house, prepared a feast, and invited everyone to come and eat. She represented everything good, true, and life-giving. The Proverbs 31 woman is that same Woman Wisdom, but now she's not a symbolic figure standing on a hilltop. She's a real person living in a real house, doing real work. She is, as one scholar put it, "the human reflection of Woman Wisdom herself."

That's why the poem's final verse is so important: "Charm is deceptive, and beauty is fleeting; but a woman who fears the Lord is to be praised" (31:30).

There it is. The fear of the Lord. The very first lesson of the book, all the way back in Proverbs 1:7. The book opened by saying that the fear of the Lord is the beginning of knowledge. It closes by saying that the woman who fears the Lord is the one who deserves praise. Everything in between, every proverb about words, friends, work, money, character, justice, and integrity, has been building toward this: wisdom isn't a theory. It's a life. And the life it produces looks like this woman.

She is not a standard you're supposed to feel guilty about not measuring up to. She is an invitation. She shows what it looks like when someone takes the fear of the Lord seriously and lets it shape every area of their life, from how they work to how they speak to how they treat the vulnerable. This portrait isn't just for women. It's for everyone. The virtues on display here, diligence, generosity, confidence in God, care for others, wisdom in speech, are the same virtues the entire book has been urging on every reader, male and female, young and old.

WHAT THIS MEANS FOR US

First, honest questions are the starting line of wisdom. Agur doesn't pretend. He doesn't posture. He admits what he doesn't know, and that admission is what opens the door to real knowledge. If you want to grow in wisdom, stop worrying about looking smart and start being honest about what you don't understand.

Second, humility and wonder go together. Agur's confession of ignorance doesn't make him passive. It makes him observant. He sees ants, rock badgers, locusts, and lizards and finds wisdom in all of them. When you stop pretending to have all the answers, the world becomes a classroom. Everything teaches you something.

Third, the fear of the Lord is the thread that ties the whole book together. It's the first thing you were told in chapter 1 and the last thing you're told in chapter 31. It's Agur's posture when he asks his questions. It's the foundation of the noble woman's life. Everything else in Proverbs hangs on this: if you take God seriously, wisdom will follow. If you don't, nothing else in this book will save you.

Fourth, wisdom is meant to be lived, not just studied. The Proverbs 31 woman doesn't sit around thinking about wisdom. She embodies it. Every decision she makes, every word she speaks, every person she helps is wisdom in action. The book of Proverbs doesn't want you to just know things. It wants you to become something: a person whose life looks like wisdom from the inside out.

TALKING POINTS

1. **Agur confesses, "I am the most ignorant of men" before saying anything else.** Why do you think admitting what you don't know is so hard? What would change in your life if you were more willing to ask honest questions?

2. **Agur's prayer asks for "neither poverty nor riches." Most people pray for more, not for "just enough."** What does this prayer reveal about Agur's relationship with God? Could you pray this prayer honestly?

3. **The four small creatures (ants, rock badgers, locusts, lizards) are tiny and vulnerable, but each one thrives through a particular kind of wisdom.** Which one do you relate to the most? What can you learn from their example about making the most of what you've been given?

4. **The Proverbs 31 woman is described as a portrait of wisdom in human form, not a checklist for what every person should do.** How does reading her as an example of wisdom rather than a to-do list change the way you understand

the poem? Which of her qualities do you most want to develop in your own life?

5. **The book of Proverbs begins with "The fear of the Lord is the beginning of knowledge" (1:7) and ends with "A woman who fears the Lord is to be praised" (31:30).** Why do you think the book circles back to this idea? What does "fearing the Lord" mean to you now, after reading through the whole book?

Agur opened his mouth and admitted he didn't know everything. The noble woman opened her mouth in wisdom. Between the two of them, you see the full picture of what Proverbs has been building toward: a life shaped by humility, anchored in the fear of God, and poured out in service to others. The man with questions and the woman worth knowing aren't just characters from an ancient book. They're invitations. They're asking you to become the kind of person who admits what they don't know, trusts what God has said, and lives it out in every corner of their ordinary, extraordinary life.

Turn the page.

CONCLUSION

Let's go back to where we started.

A father sits down with his son. The son is young, probably a teenager, standing at the edge of adult life with everything ahead of him and very little experience to guide him. The father knows what's coming. He's seen what the world does to people who aren't prepared. He's watched smart people make foolish decisions and good people get pulled off course by voices that sounded convincing at the time. He loves his son, and he's running out of time to say what matters most.

So he says it.

"The fear of the Lord is the beginning of knowledge, but fools despise wisdom and discipline" (1:7).

That one sentence launched everything. It was the starting line for the entire book. Every chapter you've read since then has been an unpacking of what that sentence means and what it looks like when it touches the ground.

You've watched the father warn his son about peer pressure, about the voices that promise quick rewards and deliver slow destruction. You've stood at the highest point of the city and heard two women call out, one offering life and the other offering death, both sounding equally convincing. You've learned that your words carry the power of life and death, that your friends shape who you become, that laziness disguises itself as rest, and that the war inside you matters more than any battle outside you. You've seen what integrity looks like when nobody is watching. You've met a man named Agur who was wise enough to admit what he didn't know, and a woman whose entire life was a portrait of wisdom lived out in flesh and blood.

And the book ended exactly where it began: with the fear of the Lord.

"Charm is deceptive, and beauty is fleeting; but a woman who fears the Lord is to be praised" (31:30).

The first verse and the last verse are saying the same thing. Everything starts here. Everything ends here. The fear of the Lord is the foundation, the framework, and the finish line. Without it, nothing else in Proverbs works. With it, everything else falls into place.

WHERE THE STORY GOES FROM HERE

But Proverbs doesn't exist in a vacuum. It's part of a much bigger story, and that story has a destination.

Remember what Wisdom said about herself back in chapter 8? She was there before the world began. She was present when God laid the foundations of the earth, when he set the heavens in place, when he drew the horizon on the face of the deep. She was beside him as a craftsman, playing in his presence, delighting in the human race. Wisdom wasn't an afterthought. She was there at the beginning, woven into the fabric of creation itself.

Centuries after Proverbs was written, a man named Paul wrote a letter to a church in the city of Corinth. The Corinthians were obsessed with human wisdom. They loved impressive speakers, clever arguments, and intellectual status. Paul told them they were looking in the wrong place. Then he said something that would have stunned anyone who had grown up reading Proverbs:

"God made Christ to be wisdom for us" (1 Corinthians 1:30).

Not "Christ taught us about wisdom." Not "Christ was a wise teacher." Christ *is* wisdom. The wisdom that was there at creation, the wisdom that calls out in the streets, the wisdom that offers life to everyone who finds her, that wisdom has a name. And his name is Jesus.

Paul wasn't the only one who saw this. The apostle John opened his Gospel with words that echo Proverbs 8 in ways that are impossible to miss: "In the beginning was the Word, and the Word was with God, and the Word was God. He was with God in the beginning. Through him all things were made; without him nothing was made that has been made" (John 1:1–3).

Wisdom was with God at the beginning. The Word was with God at the beginning. Wisdom was the craftsman through whom creation took shape. Through the Word, all things were made. The parallels aren't accidental. John wants you to see that the Wisdom Proverbs celebrates found its fullest expression in the person of Jesus Christ.

Paul said the same thing to the church in Colossae: "The Son is the image of the invisible God, the firstborn over all creation. For in him all things were created: things in heaven and on earth, visible and invisible. … He is before all things, and in him all things hold together" (Colossians 1:15–17).

He is before all things. In him all things hold together. That's Proverbs 8:22–31 in New Testament clothes. The wisdom that was present at creation, laughing and delighting in God's work, is the same wisdom that took on flesh, walked among us, and died on a cross.

This changes everything about how you read the book you just finished.

When Proverbs says that finding wisdom means finding life, it's not just talking about making smarter decisions. It's pointing, whether it fully knew it or not, toward the one who said, "I am the way, the truth, and the life" (John 14:6).

When Proverbs says that wisdom built her house and prepared a feast and invited everyone to come and eat, it's painting a picture that Jesus would later fill in with his own words: "Come to me, all you who are weary and burdened, and I will give you rest" (Matthew 11:28).

When Proverbs says that wisdom was there at the beginning, holding the universe together, it's whispering a truth that the New Testament shouts from the rooftops: Jesus Christ is the wisdom of God, and everything that exists was made through him and for him and holds together in him.

The book of Proverbs isn't just a collection of good advice. It's a signpost. And every signpost in it points to the same person.

WHAT NOW?

So where does that leave you? You're probably not a king in ancient Israel. You're probably not making decisions about national policy or choosing between rival empires. You're young. You're navigating school and friendships and family and a world that's more complicated than it's ever been. You're trying to figure out who you are and who you want to become.

Proverbs was written for exactly that moment.

The choices you make right now, the ones that feel small and ordinary, are building something. Every time you tell the truth when a lie would be easier, you're laying a brick. Every time you bite your tongue instead of saying the cruel thing, you're laying a brick. Every time you choose a friend who sharpens you over one who flatters you, show up for the work nobody applauds, refuse to let envy rot your bones, or stand up for someone who can't stand up for themselves, you're laying a brick.

You're building a life. And the foundation matters more than the blueprints.

The fear of the Lord is that foundation. Not fear as in terror, but fear as in taking God seriously. Believing that he is real, that he made the world, that he knows how life works, and that his way is better than yours even when yours feels easier. That's the starting line. That's where wisdom begins. And according to the New Testament, that's where you meet Jesus, because he is wisdom itself, standing at the crossroads, calling out to anyone who will listen.

Proverbs has given you the framework. It's shown you what wisdom looks like in your words, your friendships, your work, your character, and your sense of justice. It's warned you about the voices that will try to pull you off course and introduced you to the voice that will lead you home.

Now you have to choose which voice to follow.

The father has said everything he can say. Wisdom has shouted from the highest point of the city. The feast is prepared. The invitation has been given.

The rest is up to you.

www.ingramcontent.com/pod-product-compliance
Lightning Source LLC
Chambersburg PA
CBHW051001050726

47592CB00007B/2665